JUST DESIGN

Christopher Simmons
MINE™

Socially
Conscious
Design
for
Critical
Causes

HOW
BOOKS

Cincinnati, Ohio
www.howdesign.com

ISBN: 978-1-60061971-7

For more excellent books and resources for designers, visit www.howdesign.com.

15 14 13 12 11   5 4 3 2 1

Distributed in Canada by Fraser Direct
100 Armstrong Avenue
Georgetown, Ontario, Canada L7G 5S4
Tel: (905) 877-4411

Distributed in the U.K. and Europe by F&W Media International, LTD
Brunel House, Forde Close, Newton Abbot, TQ12 4PU, UK
Tel: (+44) 1626 323200, Fax: (+44) 1626 323319
Email: enquiries@fwmedia.com

Distributed in Australia by Capricorn Link
P.O. Box 704, Windsor, NSW 2756 Australia
Tel: (02) 4577-3555

media

Edited by Amy Owen
Designed by MINE™, San Francisco | www.minesf.com
Art directed by Grace Ring
Inside front cover t-shirt by Andreu Osika, Artefacture
Inside back cover by Anonymous
Production coordinated by Greg Nock

ACKNOWLEDGMENTS
This book would neither be possible nor good without the talent, encouragement, contribution
and support of the following people, whose contributions I acknowledge with thanks and humility:

Brian Collins, who told me to write it.

Tom Biederbeck, who spent two years quietly making me a better writer.

**Kate Andrews, John Bielenberg, Alice Bybee, Brian Dougherty, Mike Fretto, Ric Grefé,
Josh Higgins, Randy J. Hunt, Kalle Lasn, Michael Osborne, Emily Pilloton, Aaris Sherin,
Brian Singer, Alissa Walker** and **Cinthia Wen,** whose writing and insight provide critical
substance to these pages and my life.

The many contributors (both published and omitted) whose work and deeds are the substance
and inspiration for the book.

My staff, including **Ethan Davis, Matthew Delbridge, Justin Holbrook, Reena Karia** and
Nathan Sharp, whose talent and intelligence are manifest throughout; with special thanks to
Tim Belonax for his substantial contribution to the design and character of the book.

My editor, **Amy Owen,** whose patience, encouragement and support rescued this project more
than once and whose oversight made it measurably better.

Grace Ring, for her keen eye and helpful feedback.

Lauren Bailey, whose attentive fact-checking and thoughtful copyediting was indispensable.

HOW Books, for believing, as I believe, that this book represents the right idea at the right time.

My parents, for everything, starting from the beginning.

My wife, **Amelie Wen,** and two boys, **Baker** and **Canon,** whose patience, support and love
sustain all efforts, but were especially tested on this one.

Gavin Newsom

Lt. Governor of California

"Designers are the mediators of our daily experience. The easier my compost bucket is to use, the more comfortable my ride on the bus, and the more appealing my reusable grocery bag, the more likely I am to participate in environmentally sound practices. Designers carry a heavy responsibility, but at the same time they can offer our future the greatest gift."

CONTENTS

John Bielenberg

Founder, Project M
Co-founder, C2 LLC,
COMMON

FOREWORD

THE BAD NEWS, THE WORSE NEWS AND, FINALLY, THE GOOD NEWS.

The bad news.
The world is at, or near, unprecedented tipping points involving climate change, peak oil, deforestation, species extinction and water scarcity. The tenuous relationship between humans and the natural world has become an unsustainable scenario. In addition, we have relentless religious conflict in the Middle East and expanding population and economies in China and India. More people competing for fewer resources is not a pretty picture. Thus, maintaining the status quo is not an option.

The worse news.
It may be too late or impossible to change course quickly enough. Humans have enormous capacity for intelligent thinking but are often victims of their own heuristic biases, or what I call "calcified synapses," which prevent them from making wise decisions that drive smart action.

So, this leaves us with three modes.
1. Pessimism, or, "It's too late and we're screwed."
2. Delusion, or, "Whatever."
3. Optimism, or, "It's possible to figure this out."

The good news.
If you choose to be optimistic, design is one of the only viable options we have. Design with a big D. Design that includes invention, innovation, human ingenuity and creative problem solving through design thinking and execution.

I believe that most designers are optimistic and passionate about what's next, not what's now or what's been. This makes them unlike politicians, religious leaders or most corporate executives who are largely acting to protect the power or resources that they already have accumulated. The future will be defined more by what we do now than what we did before.

Now is the time for designers to step up and use what they know how to do to help shape a positive future for people and the planet.

Christopher C.H. Simmons

Creative Director, MINE™
Adjunct Professor of Design, CCA
Past President, AIGA SF

INTRODUCTION

Most design books fall into one of two categories: One is the lush visual catalog of work that reproduces well at a small size, crammed three, four, six to a page with little to no analysis save for the occasional interruption of a case study. The other is the thoughtful academic tome, packed with margin-to-margin text and devoid of visual context. This book is committed to being neither.

This is a book designed to be read as well as looked at. It is a book you can take your time with, return to and share. If you are a designer it is offered as an inspirational nudge, the gentle force of which I hope is sufficient to alter, however slightly, the creative trajectory you may be following. If you are not (or not yet) a designer, it is my hope to share with you a highly necessary, evolving and satisfying segment of a diverse profession.

Just design.
Designers frequently describe themselves as "problem-solvers." We apply our creative talents to finding new and appropriately innovative solutions to common questions. These questions may include how to best articulate a corporate brand, how to connect with a particular audience or how to communicate across cultural boundaries. Sometimes the question may just be about how to sell the most widgets. Each of these are worthy pursuits and each involves a certain kind of problem solving—what Charles Eames described as "design addressing itself to the need." But now—just as in any age—there are problems that are larger than brands and consumers (and widgets). There are needs as fundamental as equality, water, education, community, peace, justice and hope. As designers, we work according to own interests and values (and/or those of our clients). When and where these motivations intersect with thoseof the broader profession and (more importantly) society as a whole, we realize the potential for our work to both be and *do* good. When design benefits more than the double bottom line it achieves a laudable standard. With more than a hint of righteousness, one might call it "just."

PHOTO: Nathan Sharp

Just design.

This is not to suggest that so-called "good" design is necessarily better design; bus schedules, product labels, freeway signs and ballots are all critical elements of our designed society. In these experiences there can be no righteousness. They are, importantly, neutral. Nevertheless, they require skillful design—just as the most mundane products and incidental experiences must also be designed. Collectively these fabricate the visual landscape of our culture. In the same manner that ancient societies adorned their buildings, vases and public spaces with frescoes, statuary and other art, our contemporary visual culture is a tableau of separate designed experiences coalesced into a patchwork landscape of commercial art.

In this context the average person is much more likely to interact with a cereal box than an annual report for a nonprofit organization. We are more frequently engaged by warning labels than we are by earnestly-crafted manifestos. Yet given the choice between designing birth control packaging or a poster promoting safer sex, most designers will opt for the latter.

In a 2010 interview on the blog pretty classy, designer Paula Scher lamented that today's young designers have largely abandoned their roles as improvers of our general visual environment, asserting that many "only want to work on cultural work, or not-for-profit work, or on projects they perceive as 'good-for-society.'" She goes on to say that these designers are encouraged to shun mainstream corporate work by the way design is being taught in design schools and grad programs, and by the attention that the professional community lavishes on well-meaning but otherwise esoteric projects. Though I disagree with her final assertion, I share her concern that books like this one may seem to elevate "good" design to a mantle above that of design which seeks to do anything less than save the world. Any inference that the projects included here are more noble or more worthy than the more vernacular work of our profession would be to misread the intention of this book. Its purpose is to celebrate the best of cause-based design, not to marginalize the very necessary work most designers do every day. Whether for greater good or greater profit, it's all just design.

Just design.

Another way to consider this title is as an imperative. Among the many inspirations I have drawn from the researching and writing this book is the importance of simply *doing* something. No matter what the cause or goal, and irrespective of whether the projects were client- or designer-initiated, the success of these projects invariably stems from an eagerness to work. In a time of complexity, uncertainty and unbridled acceleration, it has become increasingly necessary to participate through swift, thoughtful, nimble action. To quote Debbie Millman, "We can talk about making a difference, we can make a difference, or we can do both." Or, to paraphrase, "Just design."

Christopher Simmons is a designer, writer, educator, design advocate and principal of the noted San Francisco design office, MINE™. MINE™ designs identities, books, products, packaging and print and interactive campaigns for some of the world's leading influencers and foremost thinkers in both the commercial and nonprofit sectors.

Christopher's previous books include *LogoLab*, *Letterhead & Logo Design 9* and *Color Harmony: Logos*. He has written for AIGA, *Create*, *HOW* magazine, Monster.com and *STEP*, as well as several blogs, including his own. He lectures on design issues for colleges, universities and professional associations, and frequently participates as a judge for major national and international competitions. Christopher is an Advisor to Project M and an adjunct professor of design at the California College of the Arts (CCA), where he also sits on the Senior Thesis Committee.

Christopher is a past president of AIGA San Francisco. On completion of his tenure in that role, then-Mayor Gavin Newsom issued an official proclamation declaring San Francisco to be a city "where design makes a difference."

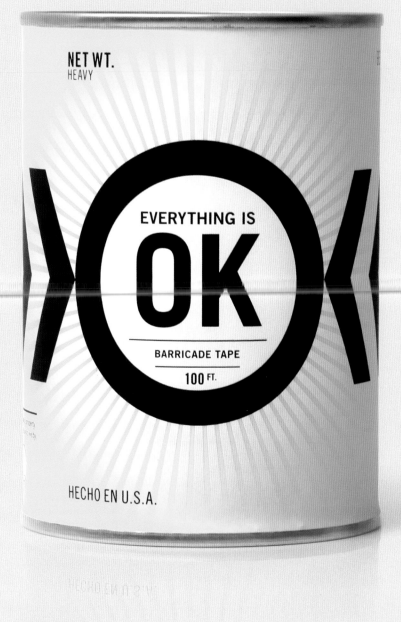

NET WT.
HEAVY

EVERYTHING IS

OK

BARRICADE TAPE

100 FT.

HECHO EN U.S.A.

Everything is OK
MINE™ SAN FRANCISCO, CALIFORNIA

CREATIVE DIRECTOR Christopher Simmons
DESIGNERS Christopher Simmons, Tim Belonax

CLIENT Everyone

WHY YOU SHOULD CARE   Good behavior is the last refuge of mediocrity.
(Henry Haskins)

◄ **Everything is OK**

Everything is OK began as a simple project in our studio. Reacting to the mounting inequities in our world and culture, we set out to assemble a list of resources that would point people toward positive action. We built a website (everythingisok.com) as a means of sharing these links. To promote the site, we designed barricade tape with the incongruous message, "everything is ok."

The tape was first deployed during the 2006 U.S. election, and then again during a massive pillow fight in San Francisco. The response to the tape was overwhelming, and we soon realized that people were more interested in the tool we had created than the project it was designed to promote. It started showing up in magazines, museum collections, books and blogs People called and emailed asking for tape of their own. Gradually, we became interested in exploring the possibilities represented by this intersection of design, art and activism.

"Everything is OK" can be read as an affirming phrase or as a condemning indictment of mediocrity—a tension that is amplified when the message delivered through the cautionary medium of barricade tape. Deployed, the message garners additional layers of meaning—taking on new life and relevance as an interactive caption that modifies spaces, objects and events.

We continue to produce and distribute the signature tape, but the project has expanded to include other artifacts. In 2009, we created a conceptual storefront for the San Francisco Arts Commission, and we have begun producing a series of posters by various artists, each offering their unique take on the enigmatic phrase.

REALM

2011/2012

◄ REALM Charter School

REALM is Berkeley's first and only charter school. The name, an acronym for Revolutionary Education and Learning Movement, was the inspiration for the identity. The school's founder, Robert Redford Foundation honoree Victor Diaz, outlined a visionary plan for a truly 21st century school. Based around principles of Design Thinking, REALM represents a radical departure from the educational status quo. The student-centered curriculum is heavily community- and project-based, and was corroboratively developed among faculty, parents, students and community leaders.

The logo embodies this progressive outlook in its use of a flag—a symbol shared by schools and movements. Dramatic black and white imagery and assertive typography further communicate a sense of urgency and departure from the norm.

In a nod to the school's student-centered learning model, the application includes life-sized photos of actual students on every spread. A "day-in-the-life" timeline runs along the bottom of the pages throughout, giving context to the school's innovative curriculum. The exterior jacket doubles as a self-mailing enrollment application: answer a few questions, then fold, staple and drop it in the mail. Every application also contains a pull-out double-sided poster so students can become active participants in promoting the school's revolutionary ideas.

REALM Charter School
MINE™ SAN FRANCISCO, CALIFORNIA

CREATIVE DIRECTOR Christopher Simmons
DESIGNERS Christopher Simmons, Justin Holbrook, Nathan Sharp

CLIENT Realm Charter School

WHY YOU SHOULD CARE   The only thing that interferes with learning is education. (Albert Einstein)

Stern Grove Festival ▶

The Stern Grove Festival is a free concert series held every summer in San Francisco. Situated in an urban oasis of eucalyptus trees, Sigmund Stern Grove was bequeathed to the city in 1938 for the express purpose of providing free outdoor music to the city's residents. Since 2009, MINE™ has provided design and art direction to the festival. The design concept that MINE initiated is simple—include a tree as the central graphic element, also include people, wildlife and some reference to music. Though the general content and layout remain consistent from year to year, the interpretation varies dramatically. From folk art to clay sculpture to Yulia Brodskaya's captivating bent paper illustration, each season brings both familiarity and surprise. For the 2011 season, the designers commissioned renowned poster artist Luba Lukova to create a bold one-color design, allowing the typography to take on a more expressive character.

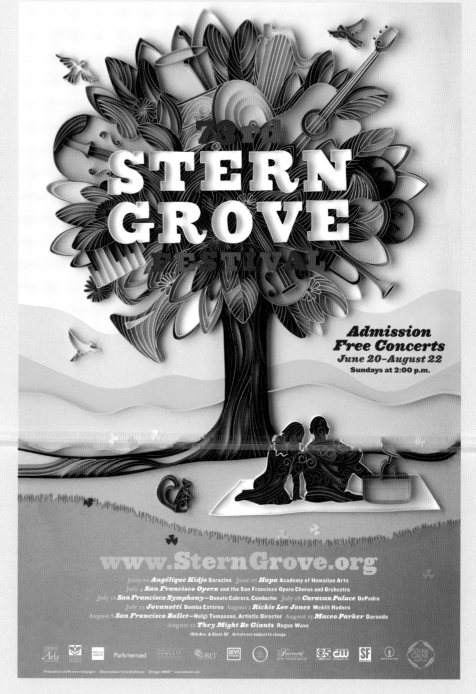

Stern Grove Festival 2010
MINE™ SAN FRANCISCO, CALIFORNIA

CREATIVE DIRECTOR Christopher Simmons
DESIGNERS Christopher Simmons, Tim Belonax ILLUSTRATOR Yulia Brodskaya

CLIENT Stern Grove Festival Association

WHY YOU SHOULD CARE If there is something to be changed in this world, it can happen through music. (Jimi Hendrix)

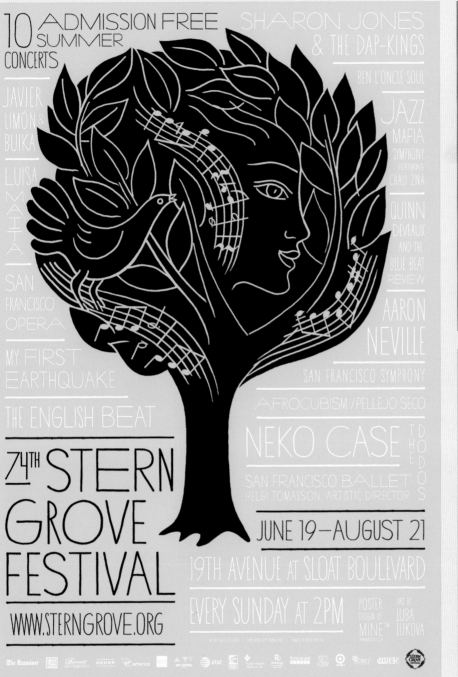

Stern Grove Festival 2011
MINE™ SAN FRANCISCO, CALIFORNIA

CREATIVE DIRECTOR Christopher Simmons
DESIGNER Christopher Simmons
ILLUSTRATOR Luba Lukova

CLIENT Stern Grove Festival Association

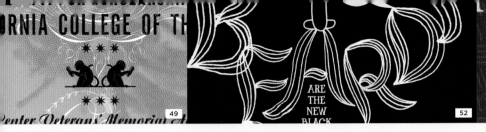

49 52 27

66

SUPPORTING
SEEKING
ORGANIZING
TEACHING
REACTING
CELEBRATING

By far, the most common way to design for the greater good is to work with an organization that has already taken up the cause. For many designers, this model is the most familiar and the most comfortable. The need is identified by the client, and the client initiates the process. The designer responds to the problem with a range of proposed solutions. Feedback is incorporated and iterations are developed. It's a classic problem-solving approach, but it's also a model that's evolving. Designers are becoming more critical participants in the problem-solving process, often uncovering new or more fundamental needs, or devising more proactive methods of support. This chapter presents a range of inventive projects—from a no-cost beard workshop (p.18) to a $488 million inter-agency collaboration (p.28). Though the scales vary, each is effective in its own way.

38

Impact Teen Drivers

Hybrid Design SAN FRANCISCO, CALIFORNIA

ART DIRECTORS Dora Drimalas, Brian Flynn DESIGNER Ed O'Brien
CLIENT Impact Teen Drivers

WHY YOU SHOULD CARE Design wants what people want. (Martin Venezky)

◄ Impact Teen Drivers

On average, every high school in California will lose a student to an auto accident this year, making it the leading cause of death among teenagers. Fewer than one-third of these are drug or alcohol related; most are the result of reckless or distracted driving. Despite strict and well-publicized laws that prohibit texting and mobile phone use while driving, these distractions continue to rise, and with them teen mortality rates. To confront this challenge, the organization Impact Teen Drivers approached Hybrid Design to help develop an in-class reader to hand out to students. The designers met with several groups of students and quickly realized that the handout approach was destined for the trash. Instead, they developed a modular activity kit, complete with posters, an accident probability wheel, T-shirts and a DVD of three documentaries, filmed by Hybrid. They also created a companion educator's guide to help get the conversation started. The overall visual presentation is candid and engaging, but the real design achievement here is the designers' acknowledgment that not every element would resonate with every student. By producing a variety of materials in as wide a range of media and formats as the budget would allow, Hybrid's smart, user-centric strategy dramatically improved the effectiveness of the project.

California Academy of Sciences ▶

The California Academy of Sciences (p.28) needed to raise $350 million in initial funding to rebuild its aging landmark building in Golden Gate Park. After a three-round, eighteen-month competitive process in which a short list of top firms were paid to design campaign concepts, the Academy ultimately entrusted San Francisco-based Alterpop with the project. Two central yet conflicting issues governed the design of this critical campaign piece: form and content. Because the campaign would be targeted to the institution's highest-end donors, typically accustomed to interacting with quality materials, the publication required a high level of craft and sophistication. At the same time, it's difficult to make the case that your organization needs a multimillion dollar donation when your collateral is over-produced. To balance these two concerns, the designers created a highly nuanced piece using CMYK, *seven* solid spot colors, duotone images and a hand-stitched binding, but they took care to limit the presence of these elements on any given spread—creating an experience of frugality without feeling "cheap." When it came to content, achieving the optimal balance was even trickier. While some in the organization asserted that the campaign was fundamentally about creating a place to celebrate and facilitate the learning of science, others saw it as a campaign to build a building. Prioritizing one perspective over the other risked alienating those with the opposing view. To mediate this impasse, the designers created a reversible cover that could instantly change the context of the content inside. Both views were given equal weight and campaign officials were given the freedom to present the academy's case in the context they felt most comfortable with. Allowing this flexibility helped ensure that the high-stakes campaign tool would actually be used.

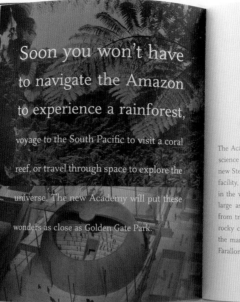

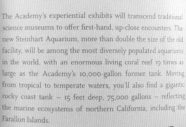

<u>**California Academy Identity, Capital Campaign**</u>

Alterpop SAN FRANCISCO, CALIFORNIA

ART DIRECTOR Dorothy Remington DESIGNER Christopher Simmons
CLIENT California Academy of Sciences

WHY YOU SHOULD CARE   Sometimes you have to judge a book by its cover(s).

◄ Girl Scouts "Journey" Books

Designing twelve books in three months is no easy feat, even for Alexander Isley, Inc. The series, comprised of six books and six accompanying Leader's Guides, was created as part of the 99-year-old organization's refocusing effort (an initiative which culminated in the controversial 2010 refresh of the brand's identity by Original Champions of Design). Each book employs a unique visual and editorial approach, yet works comfortably as part of a series. The rewritten and redesigned books aim to educate and empower the Girls Scouts 3.4 million active members and place emphasis on the twin ideals of global citizenship and environmental stewardship. The books are colorful, active and engaging – a far cry from other scouting and educational materials which have traditionally taken a more didactic, less interactive approach.

▼ H2O 4 ALL Logo

An initiative of the environmental advocacy group Make a Ripple, H2O 4 All is a campaign to raise money for PlayPumps – low-cost water pumps principally deployed in rural Africa. PlayPumps are human-powered pumps turned by a merry-go-round. As children play, the rotation drives a pump, lifting water from the well into an elevated tank for later use. The ingenious assembly is capable of pumping 370 gallons of water per hour, on the strength of just 16 revolutions per minute. The H2O 4 All campaign sells bottled water at major U.S. events and applies the proceeds to deploying PlayPumps.

Make A Ripple was founded by Janet MacGillivray, an environmental lawyer whose 11-year old daughter started her own environmental awareness campaign, also with the support of Little Jacket (p.108).

Girl Scouts "Journey" Books
Alexander Isley Inc. REDDING, CONNECTICUT

ART DIRECTOR Alexander Isley DESIGNERS Sara Bomberger, Jamie Ficker, Beth St. James, Sonia Chaudhary CLIENT Girl Scouts of the U.S.A.

WHY YOU SHOULD CARE Good design brings life to ideas.

H2O 4 All Logo
Little Jacket Inc. CLEVELAND, OHIO

ART DIRECTOR Ken Hejduk DESIGNER Mikey Burton
CLIENT Make A Ripple / Ripple Water

WHY YOU SHOULD CARE We only need three things to survive. Water is one.

Build-A-Beard Workshop ▶

As long as there is need, creative people will find creative ways to meet it. The premise of this project is simple: help real people in the developing world by putting a fake beard on your real face. How does this help? First, download a beard template from the Atto-designed website, *buildabeard.helloatto.com*. Next, cut it out, stick it your face and send them a picture. For every beard photo they receive, Atto deposits $1 in a Kiva account for a minimum of one year (Kiva is a revolutionary micro-loan charity that enables individual citizens to invest directly in projects in the developing world). So far the firm has received more than five hundred photos, but, says Atto's Heather Kerr, that's not the point, "The real benefit is that the project attracts hundreds of thousands of visitors. Now they all know about Kiva." The Build-A-Beard project took $0 and one afternoon to create.

Fair Food Fight ▼

Fair Food Fight is a campaign to promote fair trade and to educate consumers about where their food comes from. SPUNK Design Machine's campaign logo pretty much tells it like it is—the initiative is populist, aggressive and fairly informal in tone, posing questions like, "Did you know that the cost of soda and crappy fast food has been plummeting in real dollars while the cost of fruits and veggies has been skyrocketing? Did you know the U.S. Farm Bill promotes that?" The logo is just as provocative and the combination of a sticky name and a charged logo make you want to pick up your fork and pitch in.

Build-A-Beard Workshop
Atto BELFAST, IRELAND

ART DIRECTOR Peter Kerr
DESIGNERS Peter Kerr, Heather Kerr, Karys Wilson

WHY YOU SHOULD CARE A $0 investment generated potentially infinite returns.

Fair Food Fight
Spunk Design Machine MINNEAPOLIS, MINNESOTA

ART DIRECTOR Jeff Johnson   DESIGNERS Steve Marth, Lucas Richards
CLIENT Scott Patterson and Barth Anderson

WHY YOU SHOULD CARE Real food shouldn't cost more than fake food.

MEMBERSHIP
PASSPORT

buildOn

Be a Change Maker!
MEMBERSHIP IS TIED TO SERVICE HOURS

25 HOURS = *Participant*
A new member who is exploring the world of change.

50 HOURS = *Advocate*
A member who has decided to make a commitment to change.

100 HOURS = *Activist*
A member who is regularly taking action to make change.

200 HOURS = REVOLUTIONARY
A member who is deeply committed to making change in the world.

Service
DATE, EVENT AND HOURS

The time is always right to do what is right. –MARTIN LUTHER KING, JR.

I am making a commitment to be an active global citizen. I will become a leader and agent of change in my school and community through the buildOn core activities: Community Service, Global Education and Sponsorship. To the best of my abilities I will be a compassionate, responsible and empowered individual.

As a member, I will:

- Attend and participate in weekly buildOn meetings.
- Strive to contribute 8 hours/month of my time and talents to serve the individuals in need (children, elders, disabled, and homeless) and the environment of my immediate community.
- Organize and participate in sponsorship projects to support the construction of schools in Mali, Malawi, Nicaragua, Nepal, and Haiti.
- Participate in monthly Global Education Activities which will increase my understanding of the world and the role of education in the fight against poverty and illiteracy.
- Submit and track all community service hours and buildOn activity.
- Participate in Regional Service Projects and other buildOn opportunities.

_____
SIGNATURE

buildOn

AFFIX
1.25"x 1.5"
PICTURE
HERE

FIRST NAME: _____
LAST NAME: _____
HIGH SCHOOL: _____
GRADE: _____
DATE OF ISSUE: _____

BUILDON<USA<<<<<<<<<<<<<<<<<<<<<<<<<<<
BUILDING ON TO COMMUNITIES, TO EDUCATION, TO LIVES<<<<<<<<

◄ buildOn Passport

buildOn is a nonprofit organization that empowers primarily urban U.S. high school students through classroom and after-school programs. In addition to serving their own neighborhoods and communities, buildOn youths strive to end the crippling cycle of illiteracy, poverty and low expectations by actually building schools that bring literacy to children and adults in developing countries. Supporting these aims, New York-based Courtney & Co. designed the buildOn passport—a pocket-sized, passport-style document that allows students to personally track their volunteer time and services. "The idea was to create a stronger experience of membership," says Courtney & Co.'s Wendy Hu, "The passport creates a sense of belonging to something bigger and keeps students motivated to continue giving."

Working on the buildOn passport both inspired and motivated the designers. After completing the project, the team held a fund-raiser at their office, then matched the proceeds by donating a portion of their billings. They raised enough money to build a school in Mali—and traveled there to help build it. The designers have since deepened their relationship with buildOn, partnering on several new projects and traveling to Nicaragua with the organization's founder to capture more incredible stories there.

buildOn Passport
Courtney & Co. NEW YORK, NEW YORK

ART DIRECTOR Suzi Speedling DESIGNER Wendy Hu
CLIENT buildOn

WHY YOU SHOULD CARE Good design motivates. (Otl Aicher)

"Citizen Scholar describes not only who I am but who I strive to be and who I want to be around."

RANDY J. HUNT

RANDY J. HUNT IS THE FOUNDER OF CITIZEN SCHOLAR, a Brooklyn-based design studio committed to working with clients who care as much about the big picture as he does. He is also the cofounder of Supercorp, a software company whose e-commerce engine powers the community marketplace Supermarket. Hunt writes and lectures on design responsibility and other issues, and is a frequent guest critic at colleges and universities. His writing and interviews have appeared in *Print* magazine, *Massive Change*, *VOICE AIGA Journal of Design*, *Lemon* magazine and elsewhere.

Randy J. Hunt
Citizen Scholar BROOKLYN, NEW YORK
Photo: Christopher Simmons

You describe Citizen Scholar as a "responsible design studio." What does that mean, exactly? The first part of being responsible is being aware. After that, it's making choices based on the information that awareness provides. The projects we touch affect people and use resources, for better or worse. Responsible design places a high priority on skewing things toward the better side of the equation.

I've always thought about it as an aspiration and personal challenge. Citizen Scholar describes not only who I am but who I strive to be and who I want to be around.

Have you always been a responsible designer? If not, what changed you? I think responsibility is less about being a designer and more about how I behave as one human being to other human beings. That informs how I approach design, but I'd like to think it informs how I do everything else, too. I credit my family and teachers for instilling that in me.

Are there irresponsible design studios? Describe them. Definitely! I think we all fall on a scale that ranges between good and bad when it comes to our choices. I know some design firms that have grown too big and have high overhead. That kind of overhead changes the decision-making process. We should absolutely be running profitable design businesses, but profitable doesn't have to mean continuous growth.

How are you able to sustain your studio working mostly for artists, non-profits and other typically underfunded groups? There are many ways to think about sustainability. For example, currently, I'm the interaction design director at Etsy.com. We're working to rewrite the story of how people acquire products in a way that allows them to know who makes the things they buy and where those things come from. Previously, I cofounded a marketplace that helps independent designers and artists market and sell their work. These roles, in addition to the studio's client work, self-initiated work, writing, consulting and other design-related activities add up to a complete and sustaining experience, both professionally and personally.

Where do you draw the line? For me, the first line is at the personal level. Then there is a secondary line at the subject matter/project/client level. I avoid working for people I don't genuinely like and respect. It tends to be that the people I enjoy being around share a similar sense of responsibility when it comes to their work and how it should enter the world. It's a natural extension that the projects they're involved in line up with Citizen Scholar's goals. There are also plenty of nonprofits and other groups that misuse resources and are fundamentally ineffective. Design can't help them, so I'd say I draw the line there.

Why? When everyone involved in a project is engaged and our interests are aligned, it's much more likely we'll do a good job, enjoy the process and the outcome, and feel proud about what the work means to other people. If the cards are stacked against that before a project even starts, then it's a bad use of everyone's energy and talent. We don't want pats on the back for being "responsible designers." We simply want to live with the best experience of life we possibly can and help make that happen for other people too.

Pentagram Cigarette Packaging ▶

Contrast these two approaches to curbing tobacco use. On this page is a proposal by Pentagram's DJ Stout as to how Big Tobacco could comply with the Obama administration's 2009 legislation requiring that full color cigarette ads be replaced with black-and-white only text. Stout was asked by friend and *St. Petersburg Times* reporter Chris Kozlowski how he would advise a major tobacco company like Marlboro to work with the new restrictions. His response, which was featured in Kozlowski's June 2009 article, was both brilliant and contrarian: "Our marketing advice to cigarette companies in the new heavily-regulated era is to fully accept the aggressive antismoking restrictions and to wallow in the government's apocalyptic health warnings. Don't make excuses … just transform the whole cigarette pack into a three-dimensional warning label."

That recommendation is visualized in the series of hypothetical package redesigns pictured here. Though unmistakably deadly in tone, the packaging is still attractive, treading a tenuous line between commerce and compliance, sincerity and satire.

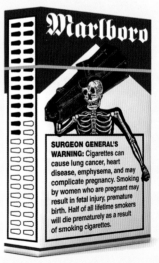

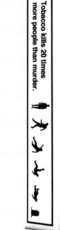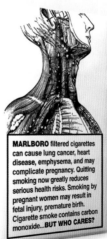

Pentagram Cigarette Packaging
Pentagram AUSTIN, TEXAS

ART DIRECTOR DJ Stout DESIGNER Carla Rogers
CLIENT St. Petersburg Times

WHY YOU SHOULD CARE The ugly truth can also be beautiful.

◄ **World No Tobacco Day Campaign**

In a project for the United Nations' World Health Organization, design firm Fabrica took an even more aggressive approach. While the new American restrictions on tobacco advertising are strict by U.S. standards, several other countries, including the UK and Canada, have even more restrictive laws, requiring much more explicit warnings and/or graphic images of the negative effects of smoking. The pictorial warnings are among the most effective, reducing tobacco use by approximately 15% in the countries where that system is implemented. The images are coarse and extremely disturbing, leaving no ambiguity about the harmful consequences of tobacco use.

Both projects seek to engage with legislation designed to curb the use of tobacco, but there are nuances to each brief that define different creative outcomes and results.

World No Tobacco Day Campaign

Fabrica TREVISO, ITALY

CREATIVE DIRECTOR Omar Vulpinari ART DIRECTORS Namyoung An, Gabriele Riva
PHOTOGRAPHERS Piero Martinello, Sebastiano Scattolin CLIENT UNWHO

WHY YOU SHOULD CARE Sometimes, the truth is ugly.

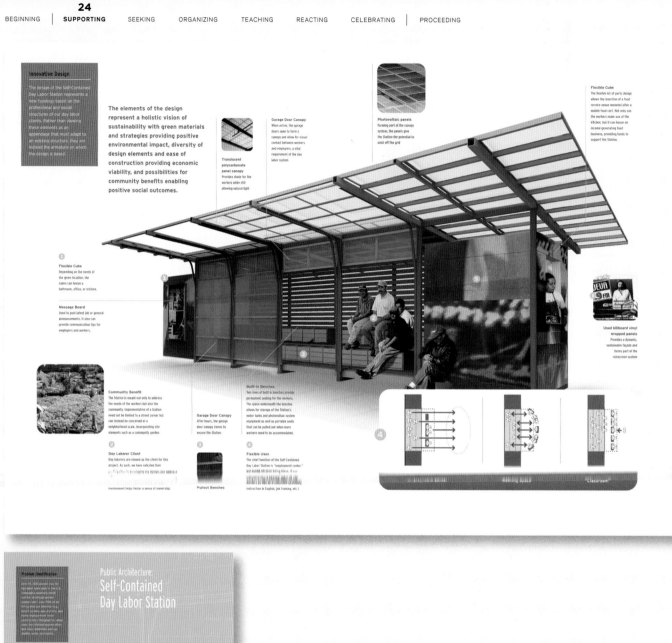

Innovative Design

The design of the Self-Contained Day Labor Station represents a new typology based on the professional and social structures of our day labor clients. Rather than viewing these elements as an appendage that must adapt to an existing structure, they are instead the armature on which the design is based.

The elements of the design represent a holistic vision of sustainability with green materials and strategies providing positive environmental impact, diversity of design elements and ease of construction providing economic viability, and possibilities for community benefits enabling positive social outcomes.

Translucent polycarbonate panel canopy
Provides shade for the workers while still allowing natural light

Garage Door Canopy
When active, the garage doors open to form a canopy and allow for visual contact between workers and employers, a vital requirement of the day labor system

Photovoltaic panels
Forming part of the canopy system, the panels give the Station the potential to exist off the grid

Flexible Cube
The flexible kit of parts design allows the insertion of a food service venue modeled after a mobile food cart. Not only can the workers make use of the kitchen, but it can house an income-generating food business, providing funds to support the Station.

Flexible Cube
Depending on the needs of the given location, the cubes can house a bathroom, office, or kitchen.

Message Board
Used to post latest job or general announcements. It also can provide communication tips for employers and workers.

Used billboard vinyl wrapped panels
Provides a dynamic, sustainable façade and forms part of the rainscreen system

Community Benefit
The Station is meant not only to address the needs of the workers but also the community. Implementation of a Station need not be limited to a street corner but can instead be conceived at a neighborhood scale, incorporating site elements such as a community garden.

Garage Door Canopy
After hours, the garage door canopy closes to secure the Station.

Built-In Benches
Two rows of built-in benches provide permanent seating for the workers. The space underneath the benches allows for storage of the Station's water tanks and photovoltaic system equipment as well as portable seeds that can be pulled out when more workers need to be accommodated.

Day Laborer Client
Day laborers are viewed as the client for this project. As such, we have solicited their

Pullout Benches

Flexible Uses
The chief function of the Self-Contained Day Labor Station is "employment center."

involvement helps foster a sense of ownership.

instruction in English, job training, etc.)

Public Architecture:
Self-Contained Day Labor Station

Problem Identification

Day labor is not a new phenomenon. In the late 19th century, the dockworkers were the day laborers. Dockworkers often were immigrants, hailing from countries such as Ireland, Italy, and Poland, seeking an entry point into the formal economy. Today's immigrants, legal and illegal, pay over $90 billion dollars in taxes, yet use only $5 billion in public services. Despite their key role within our economy, day laborers are often viewed as a faceless mass. It is in this context that Public Architecture works to have an impact. Design is often viewed as a luxury, yet the presence of something tangible can be a tool with greater impact and longevity than a political statement or legal argument. Informed and inspired by our day laborer clients, the "Self-Contained Day Labor Station" is a prototypical solution - designed to be a model that can be replicated and adapted for anyone - that provides an innovative vehicle through which to advance the status of day laborers within the fabric of the community.

$90 BILLION
AMOUNT OF MONEY IMMIGRANTS PAY ANNUALLY IN TAXES

VS

$5 BILLION
AMOUNT OF MONEY IMMIGRANTS USE IN PUBLIC BENEFITS

Public Architecture Panels
Pentagram SAN FRANCISCO, CALIFORNIA

ART DIRECTOR Kit Hinrichs DESIGNER Maurice Woods CLIENT Public Architecture

WHY YOU SHOULD CARE Design doesn't ignore reality.

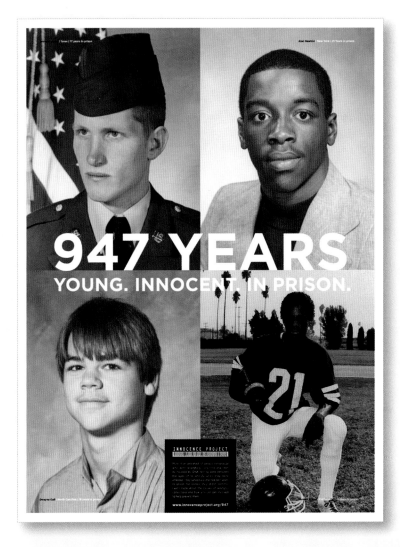

◀◀ Public Architecture Panels

Day laborers play a critical role in the "informal" economy of many U.S. cities. While their contributions are largely behind the scenes, their presence is not, principally due to a lack of civic infrastructure. Day laborers gather on street corners or near hardware stores and lumber yards in hopes of picking up work. Some wait several hours or even all day without success—and usually without the comfort of shade, a place to sit, or necessities like water and toilet facilities. To address this inequity, the nonprofit organization Public Architecture designed and proposed a Day Labor Station—a flexible shelter that adapts to serve a variety of needs. Pentagram's Kit Hinrichs and Maurice Woods created promotional collateral to help express the project's need and function. Learn more about the project at daylaborstation.org

◀ 947 Years Campaign

The Innocence Project was founded in 1992 to assist prisoners who could be exonerated through DNA testing. To date, some 269 people in the US have been exonerated, including sixteen who served time on death row. Fully one-third of those discovered to have been falsely imprisoned were between the ages of 14 and 22; combined, they served 947 years in prison for crimes they didn't commit. With the help of a Sappi grant (p.112) and the blessing of The Innocence Project, designer Masood Bukhari created the 947 Years campaign as an outreach effort to schools and community organizations. His aim was to highlight these shocking and seldom focused-on stories, to create more awareness for the organization and to help young citizens better understand their rights.

947 Years Campaign

Masood Bukhari NEW YORK, NEW YORK

DESIGNER Masood Bukhari   CLIENT The Innocence Project

WHY YOU SHOULD CARE   Approximately 50,000 U.S. inmates are, in fact, innocent.

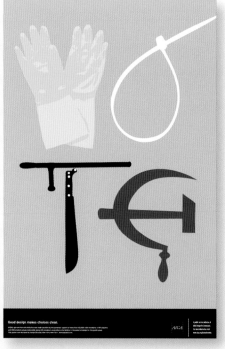

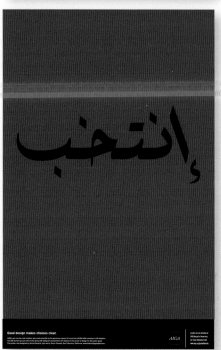

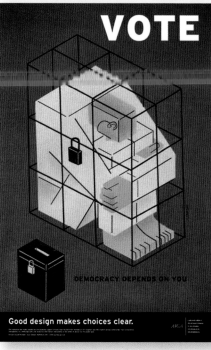

AIGA Get Out the Vote Posters

American Institute of Graphic Arts NEW YORK, NEW YORK

DESIGNERS (LEFT TO RIGHT) Office, SpotCo, Sergio Baradat, Amos Klausner,
Jimm Lasser, David Plunkert CLIENT AIGA

WHY YOU SHOULD CARE Take it from me, every vote counts. (Al Gore)

◄◄ **Get Out the Vote Posters**

Fewer than 57% of eligible voters participated in the 2008 election. That was the best turnout in nearly forty years. In its effort to address declining civic engagement in the U.S. electoral process, AIGA, the professional association for design, established its Get Out the Vote campaign. Every four years, coinciding with the U.S. general election, AIGA invites its members to design non-partisan posters to encourage – perhaps inspire – the electorate to exercise their constitutional right to vote. Hundreds of posters are submitted from across the country, any of which may be downloaded from the AIGA website. The organization also selects two dozen of what it deems to be the most effective and diverse examples to be professionally printed and distributed. Many chapters host their own Get Out the Vote events – including postering parties, exhibitions and lectures. The six posters pictured left are from the 2008 campaign. You can view all the posters at aiga.org.

◄ **OxBow Brochure**

In 2010, the Ox-Bow school of art and artists' residency celebrated its centennial as a center of inspiration for beginning and experienced artists interested in ceramics, glass, painting and drawing, paper making, print and metalwork. To help ensure a second century as a custodian of the arts, the school embarked on a three-year capital campaign, enlisting the help of People Design to create a visual experience worthy of both their history and ambition. This included not just a campaign identity but a comprehensive program of collateral, signage and amenities in support of the cause. Central to the effort was a case statement brochure which featured portraits of both the art and artists from the school.

OxBow Brochure

People Design GRAND RAPIDS, MICHIGAN

DESIGN DIRECTOR Michele Brautnick   DESIGNER Tim Calkins
CLIENT OxBow

WHY YOU SHOULD CARE   Art feeds the human spirit.

California Academy Identity, Collateral and Donor Wall

Pentagram SAN FRANCISCO, CALIFORNIA

ART DIRECTOR Kit Hinrichs DESIGNER Laura Scott
CLIENT California Academy of Sciences

WHY YOU SHOULD CARE Those who learned to collaborate and improvise most
effectively have prevailed. (Charles Darwin)

CALIFORNIA ACADEMY OF SCIENCES

Founded in 1853, the California Academy of Sciences is San Francisco's largest cultural institution and the greenest museum in the world. The new facility, opened in 2008, boasts eighteen million natural history specimens and more than 40,000 live animals—including birds and butterflies that fly freely within a four-story rain forest. In addition to the rain forest, the museum includes the world's largest all-digital planetarium, a natural history hall and a subterranean aquarium accessed via an elevator that plunges from the top of the rain forest canopy through the flooded forest floor. The museum is also an active research institute, and many of its labs are open to the public, allowing visitors to interact directly with some of the worlds leading biologists, zoologists and environmental scientists.

The building itself is a triumph of engineering and design. Designed by architect Renzo Piano, it is a Platinum LEED-certified building packed with innovative features. The most obvious of these is its 2.5-acre living roof. To build the roof, Piano worked with local ecological design company Rana Creek to invent a now-patented technology that allows the roof's 1.7 million native plants to cling to its seven signature hills. The designers built a matrix of 5,000 planting trays made of tree sap and coconut husks. The stunning natural roof blurs the boundary between the building and its Golden Gate Park setting. Other green design elements include reusing 90% of the demolition materials from the old building, the use of recycled jeans as insulation, an elaborate water catchment system that collects 3.7 million gallons of rainwater annually, and an awning of 60,000 photovoltaic cells that generate 213,000 kilowatt-hours of electricity. Radiant floor heating keeps heat near the ground where people need it, resulting in an additional 10% reduction in annual energy costs. The list goes on. And on.

Collaboration

So what does it take to complete a project of this magnitude? Nothing short of half a billion dollars and an all-out creative effort from the world's leading designers. The initial $350 million capital campaign (p.16) was designed by the San Francisco design firm Alterpop. Los Angeles-based Cinnabar designed an engaging array of modular and interactive exhibits, collaborating with San Francisco-based Volume Inc., for the graphic information hierarchy and design (p.30). A host of other San Francisco studios, including NOON, Elixir, Stamen and MINE™ continue to support the museum with promotional, event and interactive design, and the Academy's in-house design team supports the institution's considerable ongoing needs including signage, publications and of course the requisite annual report (p.31).

Identity

The new identity was designed by Kit Hinrichs (formerly of Pentagram, now designing under his own moniker). The logo is based on the distinctive curve of the building's roof, replicated and rotated to form what Hinrichs describes as a "wreath of life." The three colors represent the Academy's three distinct wings and are intertwined to express its cross-disciplinary philosophy. Hinrichs and designer Laura Scott also created a comprehensive collateral system and brand guidelines that informs all aspects of the museum's visual identity—right down to the color of the barrier lines that control the crowds that sometimes wait up to an hour to get into the popular attraction.

Donor Wall

In a departure from traditional donor recognition walls, Hinrichs and Scott created a unique installation that doesn't disclose the dollar amount contributed by each donor. Instead each donor is recognized in one of five levels, from butterfly to poppy. There were two significant outcomes of this approach: The first is the obviously beautiful contribution to the Academy's decor. The second was a 25% increase in donations and an increase in the average amount of each donation.

Exibits ▶

The working metaphor for the exhibits at the Academy of Sciences was that of a "cabinet of curiosities" – a kind of giant, modular specimen case that preserves the Academy's history in a contemporary way. The format allows the exhibits to present a variety of physical and interactive media, from photographs, illustrations and artifacts to video and sound. Since the Academy experience is nonlinear (i.e. there is no set path a visitor must take) the exhibits serve as a kind of navigation tool – attracting visitors to certain subjects or visuals, and allowing them to explore and discover at their own pace. "We thought of the design in terms of a 2 second, 2 minute, or 2 hour visit," says Adam Brodsley, the project lead for Volume Inc., "rather than assuming that visitors do not read." That approach provides for multiple levels of engagement and keeps the exhibits feeling fresh and interesting even after multiple visits. The exhibits were constructed of FSC certified plywood and used a direct-to-plywood printing technology that eliminated the need for chemical-based photographic prints and adhesives. The backlit portions of the displays are powered by low-energy LEDs.

California Academy of Sciences Exhibits

Cinnabar Inc. LOS ANGELES / Volume Inc. SAN FRANCISCO, CALIFORNIA

CREATIVE DIRECTORS Adam Brodsley, Eric Heiman, Volume Inc.
DESIGNERS Amber Reed, Margot Piper, Iran Narges, Talin Wadsworth
EXECUTIVE PRODUCER Jonathan Katz, Cinnabar Inc.
CLIENT The California Academy of Sciences

WHY YOU SHOULD CARE   Always design a thing by considering it in its next larger context. (Eliel Saarinen)

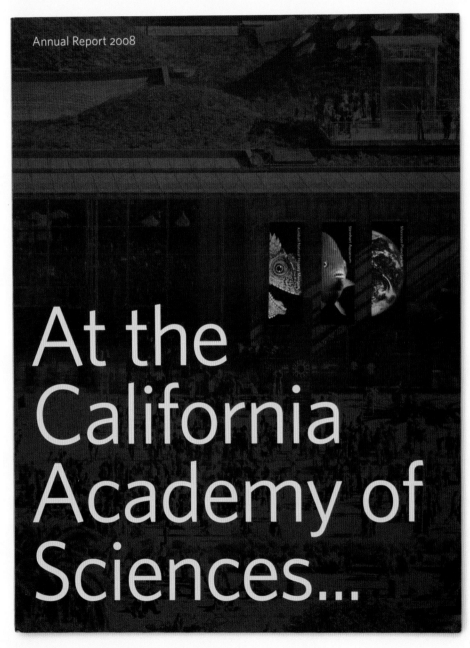

Annual Report 2008

At the
California
Academy of
Sciences...

◄ **Annual Report**

As creative director of the California
Academy of Science, Rhonda
Rubinstein oversees a small staff
of in-house designers and directs
outside collaborations. Running
up to the Academy's opening, she
and her team, including interns
Emily Craig and Jennifer Hennesy
from the California College of the
Arts, created much of the interior
signage and informational materials
for the venue. Parallel to this effort,
Rubinstein was also charged with
creating the institution's first annual
report under the new identity, an
effort she describes as challenging,
but ultimately rewarding. In addition
to its required financial reporting,
the report served as one of the
first promotional showcases of the
new facility—highlighting its many
compelling components with a clear,
clean and bold design. As the first
high-profile publication to come
out of the re-launched institution,
Rubinstein's Annual Report set the
tone for the suite of publications
and materials to follow.

Naturally, the report uses 100%
post-consumer recycled paper and
was printed with VOC-free and
low-VOC inks.

California Academy of Sciences Annual Report
California Academy of Sciences SAN FRANCISCO, CALIFORNIA

ART DIRECTOR Rhonda Rubinstein DESIGNER Andrew McCormick
CLIENT California Academy of Sciences

WHY YOU SHOULD CARE   The beginning is the most important part of the work. (Plato)

Narrative Poster Project ▶

The narrative poster project was developed for the Citymine(d) Micronomics Festival, in Brussels. Micronomics centers around how individuals can create small, experimental exchanges at the neighborhood level to address issues such as food production, local economics, land use and waste disposal. The promotional poster series presents themed fictional narratives based on neighborhoods where the festival workshops were to take place. The sequenced poster series was presented in the twelve languages most commonly spoken in Brussels — Dutch, French, Turkish, Italian, Russian, Greek, German, Portuguese, Lingala, Arabic, Spanish and English.

Red Flag Campaign ▶▶

Created for the Virginia Sexual & Domestic Violence Action Alliance (VSDVAA), the Red Flag Campaign was Virginia's first statewide public awareness campaign to promote the prevention of dating violence on college campuses. The campaign began by strategically placing small red flags imprinted with handwritten messages on and around college campuses. With no explanation, the ambiguous flags captured attention and generated conversation. The second phase located the flags in photographic posters, providing context and further relevance to the message. Faculty and staff were also provided a handbook to help further awareness and intervention. The posters pointed viewers to a website containing resources and facts surrounding the often overlooked area of dating violence. The campaign was so successful that it's now being launched nationwide.

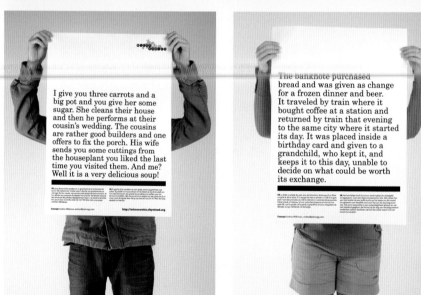

Narrative Poster Project, Brussels

Andrea Wilkinson HAMILTON, NEW ZEALAND

DESIGNER Andrea Wilkinson

WHY YOU SHOULD CARE   Little things make big things happen.

Red Flag Campaign

Another Limited Rebellion RICHMOND, VIRGINIA

DESIGNER Noah Scalin
CLIENT Virginia Sexual & Domestic Violence Action Alliance (VSDVAA)

WHY YOU SHOULD CARE   The first step in solving a problem is defining it.

Gay Teen Suicide Prevention ▶

Tragically, gay teens are up to seven times more likely to attempt suicide than their heterosexual peers—not because they are gay, but because society doesn't provide the support gay teens need to deal with complex issues of identity, acceptance and self-worth. In this arresting awareness poster created for Worldstudio Foundation, designers Sean Adams and Noreen Morioka focused on that single compelling fact, representing it with a single compelling image. The iconic razor blade—presumably rendered in pink to leverage that color's association with homosexuality—is both a reference to a popular method of suicide and a seeming allusion to the common slur "gay blade." Oversized and set against a black field, it appropriately reflects both the gravity and scale of the issue. It is a succinct and powerful graphic gesture—at once beautiful and horrific—that connects to a surprisingly diverse range of contexts.

The Gay Teen Years

Gay teenage males are seven times more likely to attempt suicide than their heterosexual peers.

Isolation, intolerance and hate are the causes.

Data source: www.advocatesforyouth.org • Create! Don't Hate. Poster Campaign for Tolerance.
Design: Ashton Taylor, Academy of Art San Francisco with Sean Adams, Noreen Morioka, AdamsMorioka, Inc. • Photography: Blake Little, Los Angeles

Gay Teen Suicide Prevention
AdamsMorioka, Inc. BEVERLY HILLS, CALIFORNIA

ART DIRECTOR Sean Adams   DESIGNERS Sean Adams, Noreen Morioka
CLIENT Worldstudio Foundation

WHY YOU SHOULD CARE   One in three LGBT youth attempts suicide.

ONE
BOY.

HIS NAME IS KEVIN.

4
YEARS
OLD.

HIS FATHER WAS MURDERED.

Evan's Life Foundation: One Boy
Smbolic (formerly SamataMason) DUNDEE, ILLINOIS

ART DIRECTOR Pat Samata   DESIGNER Steve Kull
CLIENT Evan's Life Foundation

WHY YOU SHOULD CARE   We worry about what a child will become tomorrow, yet
we forget that he is someone today. (Stacia Tauscher)

Jonathan was a gang member with failing grades. After receiving funds to attend a private, all-male high school, his life changed and gang activity and drug use ended.

GANG BANGER

◄ **Evan's Life Foundation**

One Boy is one of the simplest, most effective pieces of promotional literature you may ever hold in your hands. Created by the design firm Smbolic (formerly SamataMason) for Evan's Life Foundation, the tabloid-size, unbound, black-and-white brochure is brilliantly paced, using an economy of words and images to tell a straightforward story. That story is a day in the life of one boy. On page two we learn his name is Kevin. On the following spread we learn he is four years old. In most of the photos, Kevin appears happy, but he also appears alone. That's when we learn that his father was murdered – intentionally run down by a car driven by gang members. Kevin, as the title states, is one boy. Since 1992, the foundation has helped more than 10,000 boys and girls who, through circumstance, suddenly find themselves statistically at risk. Evan's Life makes grants on an individual basis in an effort to provide financial support for education, medical treatment, therapy, counseling, abuse education, disability assistance, homeless child services and emergency assistance. In Kevin's case, grief counseling helped with his emotional survival following the loss of his father. Smbolic took a similar approach with the design of the foundation's annual report, this time collecting several stories to demonstrate how each act of giving can create a lasting impact in the life of a child.

Pat and Greg Samata are also the founders of Evan's Life Foundation, which they established following the sudden death of their two-and-a-half-year-old son.

Evan's Life Foundation Annual Report, 2006
Smbolic (formerly SamataMason) DUNDEE, ILLINOIS

ART DIRECTOR Pat Samata DESIGNERS Greg and Pat Samata
CLIENT Evan's Life Foundation

WHY YOU SHOULD CARE Evan.

Home for the Games ▶

This first-of-its-kind project is so simple and so brilliant it surely won't be the last. Through its website, HomeForTheGames.com connected Vancouver area homeowners with visitors in need of accommodation for the 2010 Olympic Winter Games. Homeowners rented their homes, and agreed to donate half of the rental fee to one of two local charities. The charities, Covenant House and Street To Home, serve the city's homeless population. The service quickly became popular with the families of competing athletes, many of whom found Vancouver hotels were either completely booked or extremely expensive. For a relatively modest $100/night, families were able to secure week-long accommodations and make a humanitarian contribution to the host city at the same time. By the conclusion of the games, the program had raised $50,000 for the two organizations, and was hailed as a model for future Olympics to follow.

Switch ▶▶

Switch is a health and wellness intervention program designed to address childhood obesity in third through fifth graders. To support this effort, the designers at Spunk Design Machine created a wellness planner and activity kit to help parents, schools and community groups engage with overweight kids. The kit centers around a day-by-day activity planner designed to help the participant develop healthy eating, physical activity and media habits. It includes a card system for tracking media consumption, stickers and scorecards to reward positive behavior and support materials for parents. The project was economically produced using just two colors, and was printed entirely on FSC-certified materials.

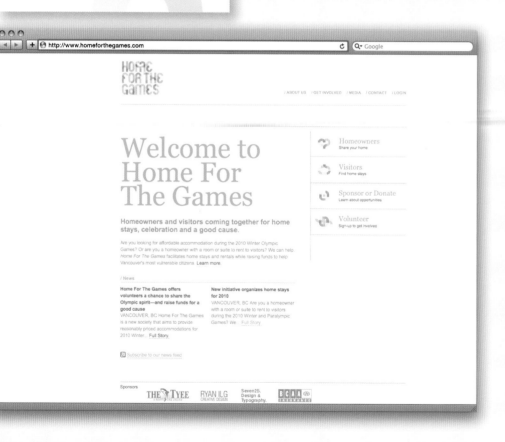

Home for the Games campaign

Seven25. Design & Typography. Inc. VANCOUVER, CANADA

ART DIRECTOR Isabelle Swiderski   DESIGNER Setareh Shamdani
CLIENT Home for the Games

WHY YOU SHOULD CARE   Design relies the kindness of strangers.

Switch

Spunk Design Machine MINNEAPOLIS, MINNESOTA

ART DIRECTOR Jeff Johnson   DESIGNER Steve Marth
CLIENT National Institute on Media and the Family

WHY YOU SHOULD CARE   One in three American children are overweight or obese.

Spoonfuls of Stories ▶

Figuring out what constitutes a good cause can be complicated. On the one hand, Minneapolis-based Spunk Design Machine has worked with nonprofit advocacy groups like Fair Food Fight (p.18) who specifically target companies like Kelloggs and General Mills. On the other hand, they work with General Mills. While it's easy to paint this as a conflict, it's also unfair to do so. Seldom does any organization—for profit or otherwise—fit neatly into a high-contrast moral view of the world. While large corporations are often (and often rightly) seen as overbearing behemoths of industry, it can be as productive to work with them as it is to work against them. In this instance, Spunk helped General Mills develop media kits to promote its youth literacy program, Spoonfuls of Stories. Not only does General Mills have the leadership that supports such an initiative, its sheer scale creates an impact much greater than could be achieved otherwise. In this example, the Spoonfuls of Stories program has given away more than 35 million books—inside specially marked boxes of Cheerios.

Boink Day ▶

The vernal equinox is cause for many celebrations in many cultures. In Vancouver, British Columbia, it is also host to Boink Day. That's the day when hundreds of Vancouver residents turn out to jump on pogo sticks (Get it? The equinox is the first day of *spring*) and jump up and down for charity. Each jump or "boink" earns 10¢ for the local food bank. The inaugural event, conceived and orchestrated and designed by Vancouver's Spring Advertising (they were founded on the equinox), raised $6,000 and received widespread media coverage. The firm donated their services and operated on a shoestring budget to create T-shirts, banners and posters to promote the event.

Spoonfuls of Stories
Spunk Design Machine MINNEAPOLIS, MINNESOTA

ART DIRECTOR Jeff Johnson
DESIGNER Steve Marth
CLIENT General Mills

WHY YOU SHOULD CARE Good design is change from the inside out.

Boink Day 2009
Spring Advertising VANCOUVER, CANADA

ART DIRECTORS James Filbry, Jeremy Grice
DESIGNER Perry Chua
CLIENT Greater Vancouver Food Bank Society

WHY YOU SHOULD CARE They didn't wait to be asked.

◄ **An Evening With David Sedaris**

Designer Bob Aufuldish teaches at the California College of the Arts (CCA). Like most private colleges, tuition is expensive. Like most expensive private colleges, CCA provides financial assistance to about 75% of its students. For the school to award $13 million in annual scholarships requires the generous support of trustees and supporters, and the occasional fund-raiser. For one such event, the college arranged a reading by author David Sedaris, for which Aufuldish designed the promotional poster and other collateral. It's a quirky poster (what is that upside down Christmas tree all about, and where did he find a Christmas tree in July?) – well matched to both the designer and author's wit and style.

An Evening with David Sedaris

Aufuldish & Warinner SAN ANSELMO, CALIFORNIA

DESIGNER Bob Aufuldish
CLIENT California College of the Arts

WHY YOU SHOULD CARE Money shouldn't be a barrier to a good education.

"I had this thought that it would be great if there was a little design firm that did nothing but give back."

MICHAEL OSBORNE

WHEN MICHAEL OSBORNE'S SON JOEY PASSED AWAY, he wanted to convert his grief into something both lasting and productive. At the time, Osborne was back in school earning his master's degree. When an instructor asked him what he would do with his life if there "were no obstacles," Osborne answered that he would devote himself to pro bono work. Within a year he had formed a nonprofit design studio dedicated to doing just that. Housed in a corner of the Michael Osborne Design office, he named the new organization *Joey's Corner*. "Everything we do," says Osborne, "is in his name."

Michael Osborne
MOD, Joey's Corner, One Heart Press SAN FRANCISCO, CALIFORNIA
Photo: Christopher Simmons

Where did the idea of Joey's Corner come from? I had this thought in the back of my head that it would be great if there was a little design firm that did nothing but give back. When I went back to grad school, one of my assignments was to find an organization in a different country and use design to help them in some way. It wasn't a hypothetical project. I actually did it. I worked with the Global AIDS Interfaith Alliance (GAIA) on an outreach program they were doing in Malawi. For part of that project, I designed these T-shirts people in this one village would get when they completed the program. Luba Lukova did the illustration and Gymboree donated all the shirts. I know a T-shirt may seem like a really simple thing to a designer, but for many of these organizations it's the first time they've experienced how good design can make a difference. It ended up being their most successful campaign ever. That experience made me believe that I could start Joey's Corner and really make it work.

Were you always this altruistic? No. When I was out of school, and for the first few years, all I wanted to do was work. I wanted to work around the clock, make good stuff, make some money and go get laid. That was about it. It's a different world, though, and I've learned a lot.

What kind of support did you have to get started? I discussed the idea with a lot of friends in the beginning. About half of them told me not to do it. I was a grieving father, already running two businesses and I was back in school. I thought about just continuing to do what I had been doing—fitting in pro bono work between the "real" jobs—but I needed to do something more solid than that. I wanted to give back in Joey's name, and there couldn't be anything flimsy about that.

I got friends and colleagues to donate their artwork (including all the ones who told me not to do it) and hosted a benefit auction at the studio. We raised $32,000 in one night. I also applied for a $50,000 Ideas That Matter grant from Sappi. That got us through another year. Now Joey's Corner sustains itself.

What advice do you have for others who want to follow in your footsteps and maybe start their own nonprofit design group or collective? Do it.

Can you elaborate? One of the things I've learned is that it's important to do what you believe in. If you want to give back, pick a cause you're passionate about, then go through the yellow pages and call up organizations that are doing that kind of work. Tell them you're a designer and ask how you can help. I guarantee you'll have a project by the end of the day. See how it goes from there.

What matters? What matters is that we do something with what we know. I've been doing this for more than fifteen years now. I know design and I know what it can do for business and for people. It matters to me that I do something with what I know and what I've learned. These organizations we're working with through Joey's Corner are filled with such amazing people doing such amazing work. People I probably never would have met otherwise. They're the people who matter. To be able to help them, to be able to do it in my son's name ... that's what matters.

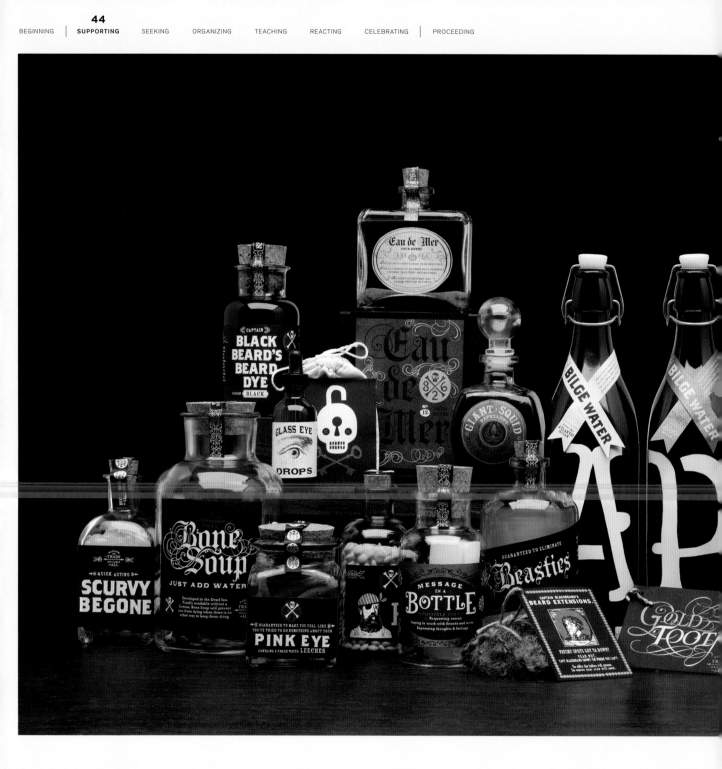

826 Valencia Pirate Supply Store Identity

Office SAN FRANCISCO, CALIFORNIA

ART DIRECTORS Jason Schulte, Jill Robertson DESIGNERS Jason Schulte,
Rob Alexander, Will Ecke, Gaelyn Mangrum, Jeff Bucholtz
WRITERS Dave Eggers, Lisa Pemrick, Jon Adams, Anna Ura, Dan Weiss,
Jennifer Traig, Ben Acker PHOTOGRAPHER Vanessa Chu
CLIENT 826 Valencia

WHY YOU SHOULD CARE It's a heartwarming work born of accidental genius.

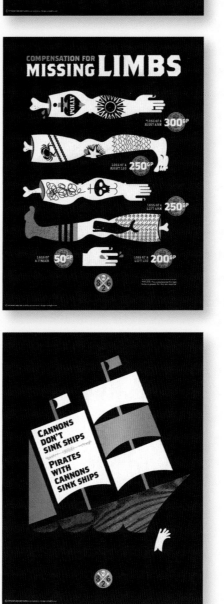

◄ 826 Valencia
Pirate Supply Store Identity

If you've ever wondered why writer Dave Eggers' national nonprofit organization is called 826, and why the writing labs are invariably tucked behind bizarre shops, here's your answer. Although there are chapters across the country, the very first 826 location was in San Francisco. That's where Eggers and teacher Nínive Calegari founded their first writing lab in 2002. But there was a problem. When they offered to buy an empty store at 826 Valencia Street in San Francisco's Mission district, they discovered that city ordinances allowed only retail or catering businesses in that area. To solve the issue, they created the Pirate Supply Store as the business front for the writing center. The quirky store soon became a neighborhood attraction, and then a national one. In 2008, Eggers approached the design firm Office to reinvigorate the store experience, developing a new identity and collaborating on more than fifty new hot-selling products for what was originally a sham business. Proceeds from the sales of Black Beard's Black Beard Dye, Scurvy Begone and designer glass eyes now help fund the center.

Today there are "826" stores in New York (a Superhero Store designed by OPEN's Scott Stowell), Ann Arbour (Robot Supply & Repair), Chicago (The Boring Store), Seattle (Space Travel), Boston (Greater Boston Bigfoot Research Institute) and Los Angeles (Time Travel Mart Designed by Stefan Bucher, p.58).

Backyard Festival Campaign

Seven25. Design & Typography Inc.   VANCOUVER, CANADA

ART DIRECTOR Isabelle Swiderski   DESIGNERS Jaime Barrett, Isabelle Swiderski
CLIENT Beat Global Heat

WHY YOU SHOULD CARE   North Americans produce 25% of the world's carbon dioxide emissions.

◄◄ Backyard Festival Campaign

Add the Backyard Festival to customized toast (p.80) and fake beards (p.18) as a means of effecting change. In an effort to pressure local politicians to enact a carbon tax, the program encouraged Vancouver residents to host concerts in their backyard, then inform attendees about climate change and the urgent need for a government tax on carbon. Pre-addressed postcards were distributed at the events, allowing concertgoers to add their voice to a growing chorus petitioning in support of the bill. The postcards were then collected and bulk mailed to local representatives.

◄ Worldchanging Book

Every designer has (or wants) a copy of *Worldchanging*, Alex Steffen's resourceful and inspiring tome from his organization of the same name. Worldchanging reports on new developments in science, engineering, architecture, business, politics (and sometimes design) that will have a positive effect on the world. Sagmeister, Inc. gets prominent billing on the cover (just below Al Gore) in a presumed bid to leverage the studio's fame and notoriety to attract new readers to Steffen's cause, though it's a good bet that many will leave the book unopened as they wait for the perforated pattern on its slipcase to slowly imprint itself onto the cover board below.

◄ Nature Rocks Logos

Nature Rocks is an engagement marketing campaign designed to support parents in motivating their children to play and explore outside. Undertaken as a pro bono effort by Los Angeles-based Chase Design Group, the identity is lively and unencumbered, existing in multiple colorways, each with a differing natural element. Those elements also play out across the website and other collateral pieces, reinforcing the sense of discovery the campaign was created to instill.

Worldchanging Book
Sagmeister, Inc. NEW YORK, NEW YORK

ART DIRECTOR Stefan Sagmeister   DESIGNERS Matthias Ernstberger, Roy Rub
CLIENT Harry N. Abrams

WHY YOU SHOULD CARE   This is one book you can judge by its cover.

Nature Rocks Logo
Chase Design Group LOS ANGELES, CALIFORNIA

ART DIRECTOR Margo Chase   DESIGNER Jinny Bae
CLIENT EcoAmerica

WHY YOU SHOULD CARE   Kids who play outside are healthier and happier. It's a fact.

Mentor Youth ▶

MENTOR: The National Mentoring Partnership believes that with the help and guidance of an adult mentor, each child can discover how to unlock and achieve his or her potential. To convey this theme, Design Army chose to take a very direct approach (and take advantage of a fortuitous linguistic circumstance). For the organization's annual report, they created a visual and typographic narrative centered around the relationship between mentor and prodigy: ME and YOU. Bold black-and-white photography and simple, dramatically scaled typography tell the story of how powerful mentor relationships make a difference in everyday lives. By operating at two radically different scales, the reader can access the information on multiple levels—from the cursory to the committed.

One Planet, One Chance ▶▶

One Planet, One Chance visualizes a United Nations Development Program (UNDP) report on climate change by creating an interactive lounge in the lobby of the United Nations building in New York. At its core, it exposes the inverse relationship between various nations' affect on climate change and their vulnerability to it. That's a diplomatic way of saying that industrialized nations are screwing developing ones. The lounge used beanbag chairs (made of reclaimed car upholstery and recycled packaging materials) to illustrate this discrepancy. Each chair represented a country and was scaled in accordance with that nation's carbon dioxide emissions. The beanbags, while also a place to sit (although the U.S. beanbag was nine feet tall!), became a kind of dimensional bar graph, each identified by an oversized eco-canvas label. Lenticular screens presented shifting perspectives of both the cause and effect of carbon emissions, and a newsprint brochure visualized the full findings of the UNDP report.

Mentor Youth
Design Army WASHINGTON, DC

ART DIRECTORS Pum Lefebure, Jake Lefebure   DESIGNER Scott Vadas
CLIENT MENTOR: The National Mentoring Partnership

WHY YOU SHOULD CARE 18 million children in the U.S. want and need a mentor. Three million have one.

▼ **Vote and Vax**

Roughly 36,000 Americans die every year from influenza. The most vulnerable are those aged fifty and older, about half of whom neglect to get annual vaccinations. In an effort to immunize this vulnerable population, The Robert Wood Johnson Foundation first needed to reach them. That's where a critical piece of data became relevant; Nearly 70% of the 125 million Americans who vote every year are fifty and older. In other words, the Foundation knew exactly where their primary demographic would be on the Tuesday following the first Monday in November. So they partnered with SPARC (Sickness Prevention Achieved through Regional Collaboration) to conceive the Vote & Vax campaign which set up clinics at or nearby polling places. Design firms Schwartz Powell and HartungKemp were enlisted to create the campaign identity. The logo, website and supporting collateral eschew scare tactics and dramatics for a more affirmative, motivational approach. The clinics were a huge success, with high participation rates—nearly 30% of those vaccinated reported not receiving a shot the previous year.

VOTE & VAX

One Planet, One Chance
ZAGO NEW YORK, NEW YORK

CREATIVE DIRECTOR Nereo Zago ART DIRECTOR Muriel Degerine
DESIGNERS Muriel Degerine, Matt Convente, Mingxi Li, Julia Besser, Mai Kato
CLIENT United Nations Development Program

WHY YOU SHOULD CARE UN reports don't have to look like UN reports.

Vote and Vax Identity
Schwartz Powell / HartungKemp MINNEAPOLIS, MINNESOTA

ART DIRECTOR Stefan Hartung
DESIGNER Nick Zdon
CLIENT Robert Wood Johnson Foundation

WHY YOU SHOULD CARE You cannot save souls in an empty church. (David Ogilvy)

Teknion ▶

In two separate projects for the same client, design legend Michael Vanderbyl brought two different kinds of sustainable thinking to the table. In a humble book entitled *Small Moves, Big Shift*, Vanderbyl encouraged the company to focus on its core narrative: creating high-quality furniture and maintaining a vigilant commitment to the environment. The first half of the book presents the company's environmentally responsible product line, showcasing the ways in which small decisions add up to a profound result. The second half illustrates how each of us, through small individual choices, can effect substantial change in our own right. Produced in the midst of an uncertain economy, the book could have easily and justifiably been scaled substantially down. Instead, Vanderbyl encouraged optimism, a point of view that permeates the book and establishes a new and stronger bond with the company's client base.

For Teknion's IIDEX Tradeshow presence, Vanderbyl again placed the company's environmental commitment in the spotlight. The primary floorspace of the exhibit wasn't packed with Teknion's modular office systems or furniture, it was populated with saplings. Each tree pedestal highlighted a different step Teknion had taken in its commitment to sustainability, and LEED-accredited professionals were on hand to share knowledge and insights on how visitors could make a difference in their own habits and communities. The booth itself created minimal environmental impact: It used 100% FSC-certified MDF plywood, high recycled-content metals and water-based finishes, and was locally constructed. When the tradeshow concluded, the booth components were stored for future use and the trees donated to Toronto's Orphan Spaces program.

Teknion: Small Moves, Big Shift

Vanderbyl Design SAN FRANCISCO, CALIFORNIA

DESIGNER Michael Vanderbyl CLIENT Teknion

WHY YOU SHOULD CARE Optimism is a form of sustainability.

Teknion IIDEX Exhibit
Vanderbyl Design SAN FRANCISCO, CALIFORNIA

ART DIRECTOR Michael Vanderbyl   DESIGNER Michael Vanderbyl, Peter Fishel
CLIENT Teknion

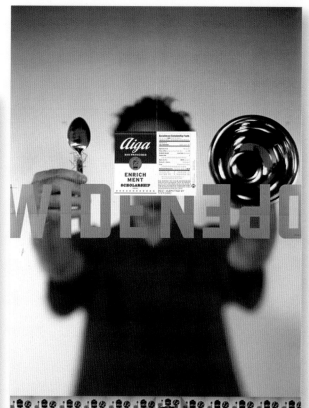

AIGA San Francisco Enrichment Scholarship Poster 2006 (above)
MINE™ SAN FRANCISCO, CALIFORNIA

DESIGNER Christopher Simmons
CLIENT AIGA

WHY YOU SHOULD CARE Simplicity is the by-product of a good idea
and modest expectations. (Paul Rand)

AIGA San Francisco Enrichment Scholarship Posters 2002, 2003 (right)
Volume Inc. SAN FRANCISCO, CALIFORNIA

DESIGNERS Adam Brodsley, Eric Heiman   PHOTOGRAPHER Leslie Bauer (2002)
CLIENT AIGA

WHY YOU SHOULD CARE It's important to give back to an organization that's
giving back.

Dáni
kúlture
Íslandá

Days of Icelandic Culture   jun 2005 – januar 2006

◄◄ AIGA San Francisco Enrichment Scholarship Posters

AIGA San Francisco offers an annual Enrichment Scholarship to its student members. Over the years, various designers have pitched in to create a combination poster/mailer to promote the opportunity. The examples here show three approaches to the same design brief: In 2002, Volume Inc. created a somewhat kitschy poster that takes great advantage of scale. A single iconic image creates the initial attraction, while the comparatively tiny label draws the viewer in. Perforated tear-off tabs remind students of the all-important deadline. In 2003, Volume reprised its role as poster designer, this time opting to use the entire press sheet (color bars and all) in a two-sided affair loaded with information. In 2006, MINE™ took a turn with a two-color, illustrated offering described as "inspirational, transformational and unattainable," a somewhat magical context in which to consider the scholarship opportunity.

◄ Dani Kulture

KarlssonWilker's poster campaign in support of an eight-month Icelandic cultural exchange festival in Belgrade included an interesting twist. The die-cut poster, representing Iceland, was designed to merge with the Serbian environment in which it was viewed; sixty-three die-cut holes allowed the cultural background of one country to permeate the visual representation of the other. Printed in an edition of 5,000, it yielded 315,000 die-cut pieces, one for every Icelander. The die-cut remnants, which featured Icelandic proverbs translated into Serbian, were saved and presented in large glass bowls at festival's many events.

Dani Kulture

karlssonwilker inc. NEW YORK, NEW YORK

DESIGNER Jan Wilker
CLIENT The Cultural Offices of Iceland and Serbia

WHY YOU SHOULD CARE   Opportunities for creating meaning are everywhere.

Next Billion Network ▶

One billion people the world over are currently connected via mobile phones. By 2012, a billion more people will join them, continuing the fastest adoption of a new technology in history. Realizing the geometric opportunity for change and impact, MIT initiated a campaign to focus innovation around the mobile platform. Boston-based Adam&Co. developed the identity for the initiative called the Next Billion Network. The program aims to empower these new mobile users—most whom live in the developing world—with innovative technologies that foster collaboration, entrepreneurship and personal wealth, and ultimately place them on a path to self-sufficiency.

Chinatown Community Development Center ▼

The Chinatown Community Development Center (CCDC) identity was created in collaboration with Taproot Foundation, a nonprofit organization focused on motivating professionals toward pro bono service that drives social change. Taproot connected San Francisco-based UNIT Design Collective with the CCDC to develop a new logo for the organization. UNIT based the new mark on the Chinese character for *people*, which coincidentally resembles an abstract house. It was a happy coincidence for an organization focused on creating both community and affordable housing.

Chinatown Community
Development Center

Next Billion Network
Adam&Co. HANOVER, MASSACHUSETTS

DESIGNER Adam Larson   CLIENT MIT

WHY YOU SHOULD CARE   Anything times a billion matters.

Chinatown Community Development Center Identity
UNIT Design Collective SAN FRANCISCO, CALIFORNIA

DESIGNERS Ann Jordan, Shardul Kiri
CLIENT Chinatown Community Development Center

WHY YOU SHOULD CARE   Good design speaks to people in their own language.

◄ Darfur Darfur

To support this traveling photography exhibition documenting the strife and conflict in Sudan, San Francisco-based Volume Inc., developed the exhibition identity and invitation. The exhibit, which features larger-than-life projections of photographs by former U.S. Marine Brian Steidle and a host of other photojournalists, captures the conflicting and interrelated realities of life and war in the embattled region. Volume's pro bono identity captures this dichotomy with a sophisticated typographic solution that is both urgent and artful.

Darfur Darfur Identity
Volume Inc. SAN FRANCISCO, CALIFORNIA

ART DIRECTORS Adam Brodsley, Eric Heiman   DESIGNER Marcelo Viana
CLIENT Darfur Darfur

WHY YOU SHOULD CARE You can choose to create something attractive in the face of horror.

The Urban Forest Project

Worldstudio NEW YORK, NEW YORK

ART DIRECTOR Mark Randall DESIGNERS Scott Pauli, Rodrigo Corral, John Gall,
Rob Alexander, and many more PHOTOGRAPHER Mark Dye CLIENT Various

WHY YOU SHOULD CARE Urban public space is a stage for viewing design in its
diversity. A mix of voices, from advertising to activism,
compete for visibility. (Ellen Lupton)

◄◄ The Urban Forest Project

The Urban Forest Project is an ambitious outdoor exhibition, with projects in Albuquerque, Baltimore, Denver, San Francisco, New York, Toledo and Washington DC. For the inaugural exhibition in New York's Times Square, 185 of the world's most celebrated designers and artists were asked to depict the form (or idea) of the tree. The result was a collective statement in support of sustainability in the form of an "urban forest" of street pole banners. Banners were later recycled into tote bags designed exclusively for the project by Jack Spade, the proceeds of which benefitted Worldstudio/AIGA scholarships and AIGA New York's mentoring program.

◄ Kitchen Dog Theater

Dallas's Kitchen Dog Theater is dedicated to staging cutting-edge plays devoted to exploring issues of justice, morality and human freedom. As supporters of both these issues and live theater, advertising and design firm SullivanPerkins assumed the responsibility of designing the company's identity and season collateral on a pro bono basis. With only $4,500 in the production budget, SullivanPerkins — used to dealing with more substantial budgets — was discouraged by how little traditional printing methods afforded. To meet this challenge, they redesigned Kitchen Dog's season catalog in a bold tabloid newspaper format. That decision allowed the firm to produce 12,000 copies for just 23¢ each — 22% under budget. And because of the lightweight, mail-friendly format, mailing costs were reduced 12% further. SullivanPerkins also learned how to silkscreen, and hand-pulled the season posters themselves. Their smart choices and generosity paid off: In the midst of a recession, they saw single ticket sales increase 14% over the previous year.

KDT 2008/2009 Season Collateral

SullivanPerkins DALLAS, TEXAS

ART DIRECTOR Rob Wilson   DESIGNERS Rob Wilson, Kelly Allen, Chuck Johnson, Brett Baridon, David Braddock, Ken Koester   CLIENT Kitchen Dog Theater

WHY YOU SHOULD CARE   Old dogs can learn new tricks.

826LA

Part of the 826 National network (p.44), the Echo Park Time Travel Mart is another of the organization's store "fronts" created for 826's youth writing program. Although each of the stores has its own humor and charm, this one is by far the cleverest. Under the slogan, "Wherever you are, we're already then," the store appears about as undesigned as one can imagine. But that's precisely the point. As designer Stefan Bucher explains, "With a typical packaging assignment, you look around to see who the competition is, then try to make your work as different as possible to break through the clutter. In this case, design is the straight man for the joke. It has to look exactly and identifiably like everything in its product category. You have to be able to look at something from a distance and say, 'Oh, that's medicine.' When you get close and read the label, you get the payoff. It is medicine. More specifically, it's leeches."

From the slushy machine's taped-on sign reading, "Out of order, come back yesterday," to the can of Mammoth Chunks that may as well be Dinty Moore stew, every aisle of the Quik-E-Mart-style store is one deadpan joke after another, thanks to the brilliant writing of Mac Barnett and Jon Korn and the equally deft touch of Stefan Bucher.

MAMMOTH CHUNKS **$9.99**

The Echo Park Time Travel Mart
344 Design PASADENA, CALIFORNIA

DESIGNER Stefan G. Bucher   CLIENT 826LA

WHY YOU SHOULD CARE   Great design isn't afraid to play it straight.

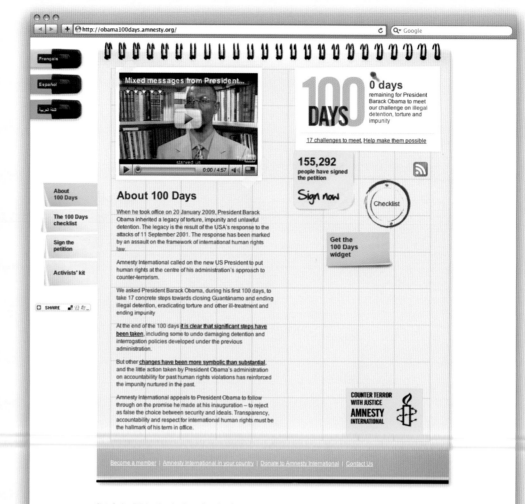

100 Days Website ▶

The 100 day mark is the critical first milestone in a modern American presidency. It's the point at which news organizations offer their first critical look at the administration's agenda, legislative accomplishments and fulfillment of campaign promises. For 24-hour news outlets in particular, it is a major media event—requiring custom sets, interactive touch-screen media walls, and its own on-air identity. Capitalizing on this obsession, Amnesty International created the 100 days project. The site was essentially a checklist of international human rights issues the advocacy organization wanted the administration to address. Developed in just eight weeks (over Christmas!) by UK designer Paul Buck, the site allowed visitors to both petition the U.S. government on these issues and access a digital toolkit to promote specific issues to friends, colleagues and others. The site, which also included a viral film, promotional banners and social networking widgets (also developed by Buck) was promoted worldwide and offered in four languages, including Arabic. More than 155,000 digital signatures were collected during its 100-day lifespan.

100 Days Website ▲

Zerofee WESTMINSTER, ENGLAND

ART DIRECTOR Paul Buck   DESIGNERS Paul Buck, Ela Kosmaczewska
CLIENT Amnesty International

WHY YOU SHOULD CARE   It exploits the predictability of the media.

Change the World for Ten Bucks, Promotional Materials ▶

Chronicle Books SAN FRANCISCO, CALIFORNIA

ART DIRECTORS Liz Rico, Nancy Deane   DESIGNER Geoff Wagner
CLIENT Chronicle Books

WHY YOU SHOULD CARE   We are what we repeatedly do. (Aristotle)

◀◀ Change the World for Ten Bucks

It took one month, one typeface and a budget of $2,000 to create the promotional materials for the book, *Change the World for Ten Bucks*. The book is the inaugural project from the London-based organization, We Are What We Do, a global social change movement that aims to inspire people to use simple everyday actions to make a big impact. The program tackles Grand Challenges including climate change, poverty, crime and inequality, but does so in an unexpected way. The book proposes fifty everyday actions that anyone can do regardless of age, ability, race, gender or religion. They range from the simple (say no to plastic bags) to the extremely simple (smile); from the resourceful (recycle this book) to the recursive (buy a copy of this book for a friend). The promotional materials were produced by Chronicle Books to support the U.S. release of the book and offered simple tips extracted for the book. The book, whose UK title is *Change the World for a Fiver*, was designed by London-based Antidote. Inspired by their experience working on the book, the agency created the now famous, "I am not a plastic bag," in cooperation with Anya Hindmarch.

◀ Politics of Possibility

The Human Rights Campaign (HRC) is America's largest civil rights organization working to achieve lesbian, gay, bisexual and transgender equality. Though always active, election years are of particular importance to the advocacy organization. For the 2008 election cycle, HRC was working on several high-profile projects and endorsements, unified under the theme "Politics of Possibility." Washington DC-based Design Army was tasked with capturing and crystallizing these projects in the organization's annual report. The oversized self-mailer format, lightweight (environmentally friendly) papers and a type-driven design helped to create a distinctive and memorable graphic voice, without looking too slick or overproduced. The self-mailer format was both resourceful and humble. The lighter weight created an impression of thrift—an assurance to members and donors that their contributions weren't being inappropriately applied to non-advocacy promotional efforts.

Politics of Possibility
Design Army WASHINGTON, DC

ART DIRECTORS Pum Lefebure, Jake Lefebure   DESIGNER Sucha Becky
CLIENT Human Rights Campaign

WHY YOU SHOULD CARE   Design is a response to social change. (George Nelson)

ma

Kate Andrews

Designer & Design Writer

A designer friend once asked me what I wanted to do for a living; without hesitation I replied, "I'd like to make a difference." As critical social issues become more closely connected to the design profession and the notion of what is "good" design faces a new set of critical standards, this is the sentiment of a growing number of designers today. Over the last five years, as I have explored, observed and engaged with the methods of how designers make a difference, I have found one underlying factor to be constant: support.

Whilst it has been a long tradition for graphic designers to lend their hand to supporting good causes, the commitment of designers working toward "the greater good" has appeared sporadic, as an add-on or alternative to a commercial portfolio, and too often considered non-profitable. Over the past decade, however, a new breed of socially conscious designer has emerged, providing brand new opportunities for design to effect change and support critical causes. Exploring design as a strategic process to affect and assist social problems, they are thinking very differently about design and, in multidisciplinary teams, are working directly with communities, public sectors and cultural organizations previously untapped by creative services in the same manner. While this new breed uses the intangible processes of design thinking to affect critical social issues and works in collaboration with the end users and client, the role of good communication design is more relevant than ever. Here lays an incredible opportunity for graphic design to illustrate its social relevance, influence and creativity.

By definition, "to support" means to carry or share weight, to provide for, to strengthen or encourage, to give help or approval, or to take a secondary role in something. In the context of designing for the greater good, supporting has become much easier in recent years. Through evolving communication technologies and the collaborative environments offered by social media platforms, we are all connected in more ways than ever before and subsequently collaboration and support is happening faster, across disciplines, and in all manner of new and differing ways.

As graphic designers, it seems immediately obvious that visual communication skills can be offered to assist good causes, but supporting good causes manifests in countless ways. Working with nonprofits, good causes and social entrepreneurs in recent years, I have learned not to predetermine what I can or cannot offer, but to think more broadly about my own skills and those of my network. Having a one-hour conversation, participating in a workshop, contributing to digital platforms, spreading awareness, joining a community, building a network or recommending the most appropriately skilled designer are small actions that help, too. Supporting good causes doesn't have to mean rebranding an entire charity; effective support can also happen on a small scale.

So, what's in it for us? While graphic design is social by its nature, it is easy for designers to become detached from the deeper implications of their work. Supporting good causes reconnects designers to society, encouraging them to think more broadly about their profession and talents, and to consider their role and influence. To really get to grips with a social issue means engaging with both the people it affects and those working to effect change. As Lucienne Roberts noted in 2006; "The first step towards trying to be ethical is being socially aware and engaged."

There are an infinite number of individuals and organizations who would benefit from the support and services of graphic designers. In a world saturated by seductive visual messages, our skills and knowledge can enable good causes to stand out, build community support and raise funds. Whether a local community group, a national charity, a social start-up, an educational program, a public service or a campaign, its sustainable success is based on intelligent, clear and consistent communication.

If we want to make a difference through design, it is important to consider which issues move and concern us personally. Which good causes stand out for you? Which social issues concern you? Who would you like to help? Who could benefit from what you do best? If you are considering supporting a good cause, think carefully about how passionate you are for the cause. Good causes are often driven by people who have a personal motivation for the project, and if you share that deeper interest with your client, the collaboration is more satisfying and the results successful.

Kate Andrews is a writer, designer and communications consultant. She has a BA First Class Honours in Graphic Design and is a Fellow of London's Royal Society for the encouragement of Arts, Manufactures and Commerce (RSA). Kate contributes to many design platforms and has lectured to students in the UK and in Oslo. Her clients include thinkpublic, Colalife, The Affluenza Exhibition, New Economics Foundation, MyPolice, Project H Design and Mindapples. She serves as digital communications strategist for the sustainability hub Greengaged. Kate was a juror for Good 50x70 2010.

SUPPORTING

SEEKING

ORGANIZING

TEACHING

REACTING

CELEBRATING

For most of our education and careers, designers have been trained to think of ourselves as problem solvers—tell us what you want to achieve and we'll come up with a creative solution. That's been our basic value proposition. But being problem solvers doesn't mean we have to wait around for someone else to identify the problem; we also have permission to *seek out* problems we want to solve. The idea of problem-seeking—a term designer Brian Collins came up with when I interviewed him years ago—suggests that thinking like a designer may be the most effective tool to identify need, rather than simply respond to it. Project M (p.94) is an ongoing experiment in problem-seeking. Emily Pilloton's Project H (p.75) is proof not only that it works, but that it may well be the future. In his essay, *Seeking* (p.70), Brian Collins explains why.

◄ **Home Street Home**

No one asked Brian Singer to do something to address the homeless issue in his neighborhood. No one asked him to care. But he did, and he does. Homelessness is a fact of life in most urban centers, but it is particularly acute in San Francisco where mild weather, lax laws and a generally sympathetic populous attract indigents from across the country. Like all controversial issues, solutions begin with simple aware-ness. That's what Home Street Home provides. Using scavenged cardboard and hand-stitched typog-raphy, Singer places his homemade "posters" in the alleys and doorways that many of the city's estimated 7,000 homeless call home. It's a small gesture, but a poignant one that creatively engages the other-wise oblivious passerby.

Home Street Home

Altitude SAN FRANCISCO, CALIFORNIA

DESIGNER Brian Singer

WHY YOU SHOULD CARE   1 in every 120 San Franciscans lives on the street.

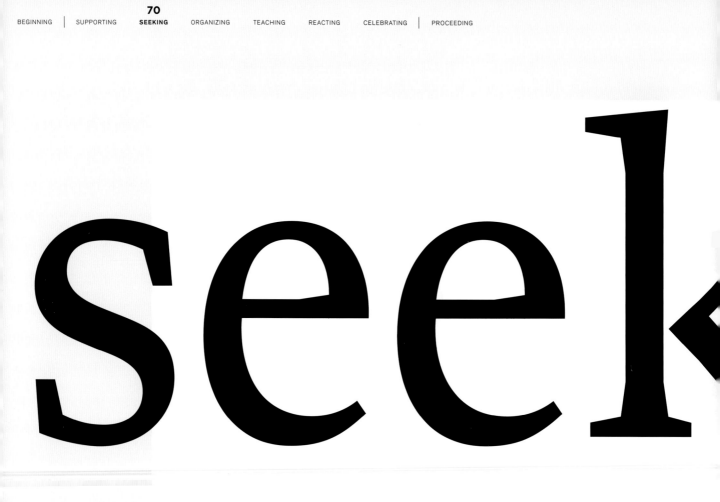

Brian Collins

Founder, COLLINS:

Innovation doesn't pop out at the end of a PowerPoint presentation. No. It's personal. It happens at the extreme margins of enterprise, where no one knows what the exact problems are because all the maps are blank. Send a designer out there and she'll come back with something nobody has ever seen, a prototype that fulfills a need nobody knew existed.

You never really know what's out there. That's what's wrong with hiring *problem solvers*— a definition for designers as crippling as it is outdated. The great problems, the ones really worth solving, aren't already on the agenda. Innovation is personal: If we are curious, open and empathetic, the great problems will find us.

The water problem found me in 2007, although I didn't know it at the time. John Bielenberg had invited me to go down to Greensboro, Alabama, with his remarkable program Project M (p.94). Project M is like a self-guided Outward Bound course for socially conscious designers. A team of young designers parachute into a poor or challenged area and then are left to discover a problem that they can solve in thirty days. Nobody tells them what to do, or even what the problem is. They live with local families, look around, talk to people, and find something they can put their hand to that will do some good. They become problem *seekers*.

In Hale County we discovered that one family in four had no access to safe water. Some of them were going to the local Texaco station with buckets because the water at home was full of foul waste from the county's biggest employer, a catfish farm. A thousand families couldn't get city water because they couldn't afford the $425 hook-up for a water meter. Getting these people meters was what the designers decided to do. They created communications and a website to bring national attention – and money for meters – to Hale County. They've connected over 100 families so far. That's not a bad month's work for a brand-new design team.

After my experience in Alabama, I started seeing water crises everywhere. Half of China's cities have water shortages and 700 million people drink contaminated water daily. The World Bank calculates that 30 million "water refugees" will have to relocate by 2020. In Mexico's Tehuacán Valley, where humans first domesticated corn, there is no longer enough water to grow corn. In rural Africa, one woman in five spends two hours a day fetching water on foot from wells miles away. There are Hale Counties everywhere.

Former NASA astronaut Jerry Linenger and I shared some of these water stories at the World Economic Forum in Davos. Four months in orbit aboard Mir, looking down at Earth's shrinking river systems made Jerry a water hawk, too. Although water wasn't at the top of the agenda in Davos, it quickly emerged as the axis that connected many of the other problems that were. By itself, the lack of safe water unleashes all four horsemen of the apocalypse: death, famine, pestilence and war. In fact, the UN predicts outright conflict over water in the next five years.

So Jerry and I, with the remarkable support of Carl Ganter with the organization Circle of Blue, invited a group of global thought leaders to explore this issue in a quickly organized work session at Davos. They already knew the global to-do list was pretty full. We needed to come up with our own resources to put more effort against these water crises. Design students are one of Earth's abundant resources, so we set out to engage them. Working in partnership with INDEX: Design to Improve Life, AIGA and Circle of Blue we invited 10,000 of them from around the world to participate in The Aspen Design Challenge: Designing Water's Future. These students would be our dandelion seeds. More than 700 students from 28 countries sought and provided 225 water solutions that weren't there before. The best of them were then shaped for venture capital and presented at the United Nations Climate Change Conference in Copenhagen.

Efforts like Project M and The Aspen Challenge are creating an architecture of participation outside of traditional silos. Today, an increasing number of influential networks of designers are emerging with a desire to make a tangible difference in people's lives. As a discipline, design is now transcending the traditional "service" roles of the institutions that employ us. Designers work at human scale. For a designer, the obligation to make life better with workable, tangible solutions is immediate, personal and direct. And while institutions are very good at making lots more of something that already exists, they are not as good at inventing the new.

Fortunately, rapid prototyping systems have transformed the designer's role. Now we can move out of the concept business and into the real-world solutions business faster than we had ever imagined. Within a single generation of designers, the cost of creating innovative solutions for small groups of people has become almost trivial. Now every designer can be a factory where the future is made.

What we can see, we can solve.

And we'll all see far beyond our office walls.

Brian Collins is Chief Creative Officer of COLLINS:, a design company dedicated to inventing brand experiences and communications that shape companies and people for the better. Brian's clients have included Coca-Cola, CNN, Levi's, American Express, Motorola, Mattel, Amazon.com, MTV, Hershey's and The Alliance for Climate Protection.

He is vice president of the New York Art Directors Club and is on the faculty of the School of Visual Arts. He speaks globally on design and innovation. Brian is a member of the World Economic Forum's Global Agenda Council.

We Campaign ▶

Inaction around solving the world's grand challenges—climate change included—is an issue of motivation and perspective. Short-term thinking is the enemy of long-term change and the scale of the problem seems to marginalize the relevance of individual response, leading to apathy and stasis. But these attitudes are inherently self-centered—too much "me" and not enough "we." That's the dynamic Al Gore wanted to change when he called on Brian Collins to help articulate his WE Campaign. Launched in 2006, the organization has grown to more than five million members and supporters online who believe that the climate crisis is real and that the time to act is now. Using custom typography created for the project by Village's Chester Jenkins, the *w* in WE is an inverted m—effectively symbolizing the shift from the singular to the plural. It's a brilliant riddle that works on many levels—formal, conceptual, literal and emotional—all of which linger in the viewer's unconscious and create a personal affinity for the brand. For designers, it in the FedEx logo of this generation: conceptual, picture and more meaningful.

We Campaign

COLLINS: & The Martin Agency NEW YORK, NEW YORK & RICHMOND, VIRGINIA

CREATIVE DIRECTOR Brian Collins
DESIGNERS Dan Grossman, Heleen De Goey, Kristina Drury, Neha Thatte
CLIENT The Alliance for Climate Protection

WHY YOU SHOULD CARE Finally, sustainability looks smart and sexy.

▲ **Learning Landscape**

Project H Design's Learning Landscape is a scalable, grid-based playground system for elementary math education. That's the official description. The unofficial description is simply that it makes math fun. Conceived by an all-volunteer design team as a flexible, scalable (non-language-specific) play-based learning environment, the space is essentially a 4x4, 16-point grid on which children play math-based games. It uses reclaimed tires as the principal material and can be built in less than a week for well under $500. Although it was originally built and tested at the Kutamba School for AIDS Orphans in Uganda, Project H has since constructed four new learning landscapes in the rural United States: Simplicity, humor and fun transcend national borders.

Learning Landscape
Project H Design KENTFIELD, CALIFORNIA

ART DIRECTOR Emily Pilloton
DESIGNERS Dan Grossman, Heleen De Goey, Kristina Drury, Neha Thatte

WHY YOU SHOULD CARE A design isn't finished until somebody is using it.
(Brenda Laurel)

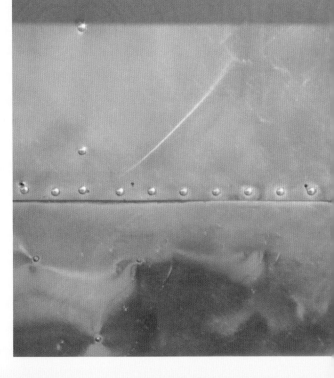

"I want designers to rewrite the rule book, cut back on the idle talk and engage the world as creative citizens."

EMILY PILLOTON

EMILY PILLOTON IS AN INDUSTRIAL DESIGNER, writer, critic and activist. She is also an unyielding optimist. Trained first in product design at the School of the Art Institute of Chicago and later in architecture at UC Berkeley, Emily founded Project H in 2007 as a "catalyst for humanitarian design." For three months in 2010, she embarked on the Design Revolution Road Show, a lecture series and traveling exhibition of forty humanitarian design solutions, housed in an Airstream trailer and based on her popular book *Design Revolution: 100 Products that Empower People.* Today Project H focuses specifically on rethinking environments, products, experiences and curricula for K-12 education in the United States.

Emily Pilloton
Project H SAN RAFAEL, CALIFORNIA / WINDSOR, NORTH CAROLINA
Photo: Christopher Simmons

Why are you doing this? Why not run a tidy little design practice and take on socially engaged projects pro bono, or focus on that work entirely? Why start a revolution? I've never been one to just accept the rules I'm given. More importantly, this revolution isn't just about my own discontent with the industry I was trained for. Designers have so much to offer, but so many of the structures we've created in our industry don't allow us to live up to our potential. There is a dire need to rethink who our clients are, what our skill sets are, and to figure out how to bridge the two to put design into the hands of those who truly need life-improving solutions. This is about considering who needs access to tools to improve their daily life—people like my grandmother, like school children, like foster children and the homeless—and putting our skills in those blind spots.

Is this really a revolution? How is your message different than what we've heard before about designing to make a difference? In 1972, Victor Papanek called for the end of luxury-driven and masturbatory industrial design as we knew it, and it is a little sad that his words are still true. I think what's needed to make a difference now is a generation of young designers who have absolutely had it with the "old way" coupled with all the tools we now have to work more collaboratively. So, yes, it is a revolution.

I see a lot of young people at your talks and events. Are you getting a different reception from the younger generation than you are from established professionals? If so, how? Why? Definitely. I'm part of this young generation, and I've gone through my own journey. For college students who haven't yet worked in the design industry, there is a huge sense of "I don't want to do this unless I can do it in a way that matters." That's becoming the norm. A generation of twenty-year-olds is about to take the industry by storm and demand new paradigms. It may be naiveté, or it may just be that there is so much in the world that needs fixing, but our generation, whether we're designers or doctors or lawyers, wants to know that our skills are going towards global problems rather than superfluous indulgences.

Graphic design is often concerned with making things that are arguably less useful than the products of industrial design. How do you think your Design Revolution principles translate to graphic design? Funny you say that because sometimes I think it's the other way around. For graphic designers, there is a huge opportunity and responsibility to raise awareness and tell stories. Product design is often a static object (something I'd like to change—to go from products to tools, from stuff to solutions). Graphic design can bring an idea to life, and tell stories in fluid, personal ways through visual stimuli. I've definitely had moments where I wish I were a better graphic designer—many of our projects could have benefitted from better visual communication and storytelling—I get made fun of all the time for using the same two typefaces over and over.

You're critical, but you're also an optimist. Tell me a little about that relationship. I think optimism without a critical eye is just naiveté. My approach has always started with a criticism laced with optimism: It says, "This is good, but I think we can do better, and here's how." It's a way of working that means you're always pushing yourself, but still content in the work.

Replate *v.* (re • plate):

To place unwanted leftovers, typically in a doggie bag, on top of the nearest trash can so that they don't go to waste.

REPLATE.ORG

Replate.org

Language in Common SAN FRANCISCO, CALIFORNIA

DESIGNERS Axel Albin, Josh Kamler

WHY YOU SHOULD CARE The last collaborator is the audience. (Stephen Sondheim)

◀◀ Replate

In San Francisco, where city garbage cans have flat-covered tops and a separated section for recycling, people had taken to leaving their well-wrapped leftovers for the homeless, many of whom otherwise sift through trash in search of food. The designers at Language in Common saw this habit as a kind of spontaneous activism and decided to give it an encouraging nudge. They did so in the simplest way: they gave it the name "Replate." The two also created a Replate logo and website, and did a little bit of email promotion to help get the conversation started. Within days, the project was covered by Core77, Unbeige, GOOD Magazine, CHOW and Daily Candy. It made the *Washington Post*. NBC called. ABC called. Then the health department called (they wanted some stickers). Albin and Kamler saw both a problem and its solution right in front of them. They recognized an opportunity to make a small contribution of talent which could yield profound results. "The trick is not to focus on how gigantic the problem is," says Kamler, "but to focus on how tiny the solution can be."

◀ A Kid's Guide to Giving

Freddi Zeiler wrote *A Kid's Guide to Giving* when she was fourteen. Freddi wanted to give some money to charity, but couldn't decide which one to choose. She began to research some alternatives but quickly found that the language on most organizations' websites wasn't very accessible to children. She did her best to translate what she found into her own words, and emailed each of the charities with a list of questions. Soon she had amassed so much information that her mother suggested she turn it into a book. They enlisted the help of designer friend Michael Hodgson who in turn brought in his friend, illustrator Ward Schumaker. Ultimately, the project took seven years before it was published, but everyone stuck with it and the guide now exists for any enlightened youngster who wants to make a difference.

A Kids Guide to Giving

Ph.D SANTA MONICA, CALIFORNIA

DESIGNER Michael Hodgson CLIENT Innovative Kids

WHY YOU SHOULD CARE Charity begins at home.

Your Name on Toast

Atto BELFAST, IRELAND

ART DIRECTOR Peter Kerr   DESIGNERS Peter Kerr, Heather Kerr, Karys Wilson

WHY YOU SHOULD CARE It is brilliantly absurd.

THANK YOU
THANK YOU
THANK YOU
THANK YOU
THANK YOU
THANK YOU
THANK YOU

HAVE A NICER TOMORROW

HAVE A HAPPY
EARTH DAY

◄◄ Your Name on Toast

Sometimes the best ideas are the simplest. Sometimes they're the stupidest. Sometimes they're both. This is one of those times. By investing one working day and no money, the designers from the Irish firm Atto came up with a way to raise more that $12,000 for Oxfam — charge people to write their message on a piece of toast, then showcase it online with a link back to the buyer's website. The more you pay, the higher on the page your toast will appear. By the designer's own admission, it's an exercise in novelty and vanity, but it works. It's offbeat enough to get noticed, fun enough to get shared and effective enough warrant a story.

◄ Earth Day Thank You Tote

I swore not to put any canvas totes or clever T-shirts in this book, but this project was one of a very few that warranted an exception to that rule, after I learned this from the packaging: Every year, somewhere between 500 billion to one trillion plastic bags are discarded. Most were used only once, but each can last more than 1,000 years in a landfill. This reusable alternative is a facsimile of the ubiquitous plastic shopping bag — and for precisely that reason makes its incisive point. It is graphically succinct with a satirical edge, offering a sarcastic jab at the same time it touts gentle praise.

Earth Day Thank You Tote

Open Studio Design NEW YORK, NEW YORK

DESIGNER Shelly Fukushima

WHY YOU SHOULD CARE 32,000 plastic bags were discarded in the time it took you to read this.

24

"Mexico is a country of a modest, very fucked class, which will never stop being fucked. Television has the obligation to remove them from their sad reality and difficult future." — the late Emillio Azcarraga, billionaire head of Mexico's Televisa

"The New Global Media," The Nation 29 Nov. 1999. 10 Jan. 2004 <http://www.thenation.com/doc.mhtml?i=19991129&s=mcchesney>.

Freedom of the Press

Brian Ponto / Lindsay Ballant BROOKLYN, NEW YORK

DESIGNERS Brian Ponto / Lindsay Ballant

WHY YOU SHOULD CARE   The newspaper will always be around. It may not be thrown on your front doorstep the way it is today. But the thud it makes as it lands will continue to echo around society and the world. (Rupert Murdoch)

25

"We have no obligation to make art. We have no obligation to make a statement. To make money is our only objective."

– Michael Eisner, CEO, The Walt Disney Company

The Keys to the Kingdom: How Michael Eisner Lost His Grip. N.p.: William Morrow, 2000.

◀ **Freedom of the Press**

Brian Ponto's self-initiated newsprint publication, *Freedom of the Press* is a crash course in the politics of information. It includes astonishing, documented quotes from powerful media moguls reflecting on the obligations of their station. Their philosophies take on frightening relevance once one appreciates the extent of their influence. Even more dramatically, it illuminates a number of media-related issues ranging from tax subsidies and deregulation to media influence over elections and the single-digit consolidation of 25,000 individual media outlets. The publication's beautiful design belies the ugly truth about the state of our media. In ironic contrast to many of today's information outlets, *Freedom of the Press* is presented with careful neutrality and very little editorialization. Instead it lets the content speak for itself, realizing that the informed reader will come to only one conclusion; in Ponto's words, "We're fucked."

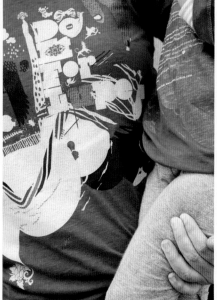

"Rosa Loves is not about charity; it's about awareness"

—Mike Fretto

ROSA LOVES

DESIGNED FOR GOOD

EVERY DAY WE PASS BY PEOPLE IN NEED. Some are our neighbors and friends, many more are strangers. Some we pass by on the street as they ask for food or money, others we pass by without recognizing their need—partly because they don't ask but mostly because we don't notice. Some live half a world away, and while we may not pass them in a literal sense, from a humanitarian point of view they are certainly passed over. The New Orleans musician who shelters strangers in her roofless home; the disabled woman with a broken walker; the Iraqi child whose heart is too weak to supply blood to his tiny 2-year-old body — until we don't know their stories, we don't know their needs.

In 2006, over a few after-work beers, Mike Fretto's friend Chris Lewis hatched a modest plan to help bring these stories to light. By using the means at their disposal—design, programming skills, passion and a little free time—they decided to start a T-shirt company with a difference. And so Rosa Loves was born. Sort of.

It wasn't until a month later when the two met with mutual friend and filmmaker Jeremy Dean that they decided on the model that makes Rosa Loves so remarkable. Rather than donating a percentage of sales to an established charity, Rosa Loves donates 100% of the proceeds from each shirt to one specific individual. Though all three actively donate and volunteer for numerous charitable organizations, they agreed that connecting one-on-one meant more to them that broad-based charitable giving. "Rosa Loves is not about charity; it's about awareness," says Fretto.

To support this model, each shirt depicts the personal story of a single individual. Their story—and their need—is told through expressive graphics created by Fretto or one of a growing network of creative friends and supporters. The

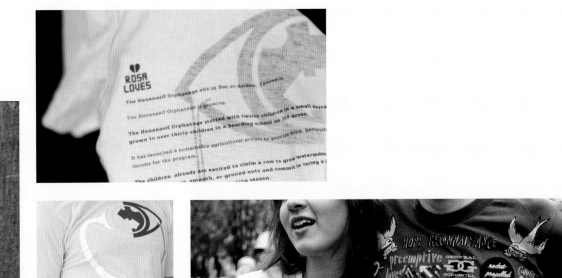

written narrative of that story is printed on the inside of the shirt, directly over the heart. "We didn't want to create a shirt that just announced to other people that you gave some money to charity," Fretto explains. "We wanted to make kick-ass shirts that people would be proud to identify themselves with and which, hopefully, would help start discussions."

The simple shirts have achieved some profound results, including funding a scholarship in Mexico, rebuilding a burned-out home and providing holiday meals to families in Florida, and presenting a widowed Bangladeshi family with the equivalent of ten years of the deceased father's income.

Various T-shirts
Rosa Loves ST. AUGUSTINE, FLORIDA

CO FOUNDERS Mike Fretto, Chris Lewis
DESIGNERS (CLOCKWISE FROM LEFT) Michael Young, Mike Fretto, Danny Jones, Tim Belonax, Erin Jang

WHY YOU SHOULD CARE Clothes should be startling and individual. (Alexander McQueen)

RUNNERS

PERSONIFYING THE IMPERSONAL

ALONG THE U.S. BORDER WITH MEXICO, you'll find freeway signs like those that warn of cattle or horse crossings — only this one depicts humans. It's a warning to motorists that illegal immigrants may run across the road at any moment. It is certainly bizarre, arguably racist, and has come to represent the polarizing debate around immigration on many levels. For his self-initiated piece, Runners, Miami designer David Garcia created life-size versions of the iconic immigrant family and placed them in a variety of contexts, each one dramatically altering its meaning. In front of a Home Depot (where it is not uncommon to find primarily Mexican day laborers looking for work) it suggests a different relationship than it does in front of a generic McMansion in a gated community.

The silhouettes are unaltered except for scale — as flat and featureless as they are on the original sign. It is left to the viewer to fill the dark void of these anonymous figures with his or her own assumptions, biases, empathies and politics. Are they running toward a dream? From the law? From stigma and stereotype? Will they ever be at rest? Do you want to help this family? Are you threatened by them? The answers to these and other questions are both personal and political and are brilliantly exposed by Garcia's provocative agitprop installation.

Runners

David Garcia MIAMI, FLORIDA

DESIGNER David Garcia

WHY YOU SHOULD CARE   One measure of a powerful image is whether it gets
recycled. (Lincoln Cushing)

Credit Card Facts ▶

When President Obama said in a speech that Americans "shouldn't need a magnifying glass or a law degree to read the fine print [of their credit card terms]," one group of designers decided to do something about it. David Gibson and Carla Hall of TwoTwelve in New York, teamed up with information design strategist Sylvia Harris to form an ad hoc design team under AIGA's Design for Democracy initiative. Their proposal: present essential credit card information such as rates, fees and penalties in the same straightforward manner that nutritional information is displayed. Their design proposal was published as Op-Ed in the *New York Times* and received overwhelming positive response – including that of government officials who are now in talks with the group about how to better use design in other government communications.

Landfill ▶▶

In 1990, Craig Barber saw a radio broadcast in which Connie Chung stated that 60% of America's landfill is due to paper and printing waste. He reacted by merging his printing and paper businesses and dedicating both to eco-friendly practices. In 2009, Barber teamed up with Designer Brian Ponto and Mohawk paper to produce Landfill, a collection of personal stories of second chances, with a unique twist. The recycled pages were pressed with wildflower seeds. Planted in the earth, each story will have a second chance at life in the form of a flower bed. By making thoughtful choices about the materials and production processes they used, three trees were saved, eight pounds of waterborne waste and 123 pounds of solid waste were avoided, nearly 2 million BTUs of energy were saved and 242 pounds of greenhouse gasses were never emitted. They also eliminated 122 miles of driving, 123 pounds of air emissions and Mohawk planted eight trees as part of its carbon offset program.

Credit Card Facts

Here is a summary of the terms of this credit card account

Interest Rates

Purchases	First year: 0% fixed rate
	After first year: Prime rate (can vary monthly) + 7.74%
Balance Transfers	First year: 0% fixed rate
	After first year: Prime rate (can vary monthly) + 7.74%
Cash Advances	Prime rate (can vary monthly) + 20.74%
Late Payments	After one late payment 0% fixed rate is revoked, and may rise to 29.99% based on credit and payment history
Minimum Interest	$.50

Fees

Foreign Currency Purchases	2% of dollar amount per purchase
Balance Transfers	3% of total balance transferred, per transfer
Cash Advances	3% of total cash advanced, per advance
Late Payments	$19 on balances up to $250
	$39 on balances over $250
Exceeding Credit Limit	$15 on over-limit transactions up to $500
	$39 on over-limit transactions over $500

Payment Options

| In Full by Due Date | No interest due if paid within the 25 day grace period |
| **Minimum Balance by Due Date** | Includes principal and interest based on above **Interest Rates** for purchases, balance transfers and cash advances |

Warnings

| Late Payments | May affect your credit score |
| | May increase your interest rates |

See below for other important credit card terms and conditions

---

Credit Card Facts
Design for Democracy NEW YORK, NEW YORK

ART DIRECTORS David Gibson, Sylvia Harris, Carla Hall
DESIGNERS Michelle Cates, Nick Spriggs

WHY YOU SHOULD CARE Information is power.

LAND

2009 ISSUE 01

LANDFILL IS AN ANNUAL PUBLICATION, MADE IN COLLABORATION BETWEEN THE GREEN PRINTER GREG BARBER, AND THE STUDIO OF BRIAN PONTO.

THIS IS THE FIRST ISSUE...

My second chance was deciding to make the best of the time I had when my sister got sick and I thought I would soon follow. I switched schools, friends and pursued my hobby of dance. My second chance was having the ability to get the life I wanted.

Mpoko Wambalebe, 24, Portland, Oregon

▼ Wind Power Logo

After completing a project for a client using 100% windpower, Mark Stress of StressDesign needed a symbol to place on the project in celebration of that commitment. When he went looking, Stress was surprised to find that no suitable open-source icon existed. So, he created one. Realizing that fellow environmentally-conscious designers might face the same plight, he decided to make his wind power logo freely available to everyone. What began as a small solution to a client-specific problem has now scaled to a simple program that supports the entire design community. For your next wind-powered project, visit windpowerlogo.com.

100% WIND POWERED

Landfill Issue 01: Second Chances
Studio of Brian Ponto BROOKLYN, NEW YORK

DESIGNER Brian Ponto EDITOR Daniel Helmstetter
PHOTOGRAPHY Luke Barber-Smith CLIENT Mohawk Paper

WHY YOU SHOULD CARE Everything deserves a second chance.

Wind Power Logo
StressDesign SYRACUSE, NEW YORK

DESIGNER Marc V. Stress

WHY YOU SHOULD CARE Do not go where the path may lead, go instead where there is no path and leave a trail. (Ralph Waldo Emerson)

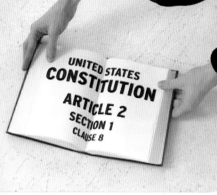

We the Constitution ►

Most people can only remember about three words of the U.S. constitution. A few know the entire preamble. We the Constitution is a series of short videos designed to bring to the foreground the forgotten words of our constitution. What began as an abstract formal exercise during designer Andrew Sloat's studies at Yale became more of a parallel passion following the riveting presentation of his piece, 22nd Amendment, at AIGA's national design conference in Denver. Some videos he completes in under a day and with the change in his pocket, others can take as long as two months and several thousand dollars to properly execute. They are all equally beautiful—presented with a spare and haunting quietness that allows the deepest meanings of the words to resonate with the viewer.

We the Constitution

Drainage Ditch BROOKLYN, NEW YORK

DESIGNER Andrew Sloat

WHY YOU SHOULD CARE   Design can help form a more perfect union.

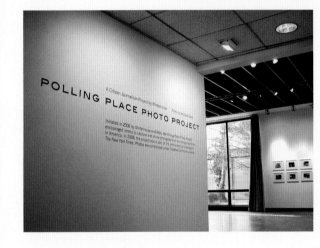

◄ Polling Place Photo Project

The Polling Place Photo Project was conceived in 2006 by media critic Jay Rosen, in collaboration with the Winterhouse Institute. Its purpose: to encourage transparency and democracy in the U.S. voting process. The project asked voters to photograph their polling place on election day—the photos were then shared via the project's website, under a creative commons license. In essence, the effort created an open network of citizen journalists whose collective efforts created a snapshot of the American voting experience. AIGA was an early supporting sponsor, and in 2008, the *New York Times* incorporated the project into its online election coverage. From its modest grassroots beginnings, the project has quickly achieved mainstream success. The organizers created the framework, partners provided the promotion, and thousands of ordinary people provided the content. Today, the project exists as a growing library of nearly 6,000 images.

Polling Place Photo Project

Winterhouse Institute FALLS VILLAGE, CONNECTICUT

ART DIRECTORS William Drenttel, Jessica Helfand   DESIGNER Teddy Blanks

WHY YOU SHOULD CARE   Democracy needs documentation.

◄◄ Midwest Seed Bombs

Seed bombs have been around since the 1600s, but became popular as an instrument of guerrilla gardening in the 1970s. Designed to deliver flowers to inaccessible locations, seed bombs are small balls of fertilizer, clay and seeds that can be hurled into barren areas. Rain dissolves the clay and activates the fertilizer, which then nourishes the seed. Though they have traditionally been a somewhat underground DIY exercise, the simple, bold and ecological packaging of these bombs have made them popular in mainstream stores across the country. The bombs are now also available in East and West Coast versions.

◄ Hogsmill River Antiques

You have probably never heard of the Hogsmill River, but you've seen it. It's the river Ophelia drowns in in Sir John Everett Millais' painting of the same name. In the painting, the landscape is lush and clear—but that's not how it appears today. Like many other tributaries, the Hogsmill collects urban debris as it winds from its chalk spring source through the countryside and villages and ultimately into the Thames. Distressed by the waterway's demise, UK designer Tom Gilbert sought to do something about it. He collected refuse from the river, built a pushcart out of old pallets and discarded wheels, and began peddling his reclaimed wares on London's famed Portobello Road—the world's largest antiques market. Gilbert bills the garbage as "Hogsmill River Antiques" and applies the proceeds to river cleanup. Though the funds make a difference, it's his public presence that most poignantly encourages the public to rethink waste.

Midwest Seed Bombs (facing page)
VisuaLingual CINCINNATI, OHIO

DESIGNERS Maya Drozdz, Michael Stout

WHY YOU SHOULD CARE Design is a tool for beauty.

Hogsmill River Antiques
Jon Barnett, Tom Gilbert GLOUCESTERSHIRE, ENGLAND

DESIGNERS Jon Barnett, Tom Gilbert

WHY YOU SHOULD CARE Society's trash is a designer's treasure.

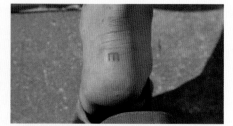

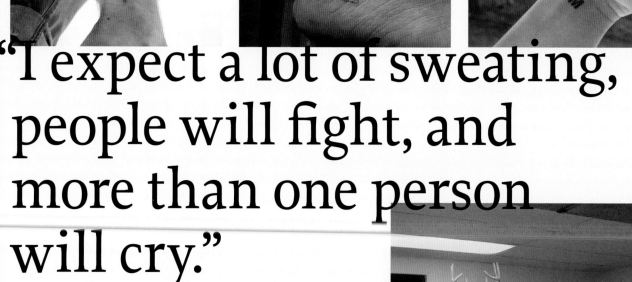

"I expect a lot of sweating, people will fight, and more than one person will cry."

PROJECT M

FIRST PERSON ACCOUNT BY TIM BELONAX

THIS IS A ROUGH APPROXIMATION of my answer to John Bielenberg when he asked me what I expected to happen in the next month at Project M. All of it came true… and then some.

Project M was like nothing I had experienced before. The anxiety, the sweat, the enormous roaches: Everyone had their limits tested. I had never felt as anxious and excited about design as I did during that one month in rural Alabama. Being a part of a group that expected so much of itself was exhilarating and tension-filled. Every day began with endless possibilities for us to create positive change within the community. In an hour, we could easily generate a hundred ideas. In a minute, they could all be shot down. It was like falling in love and then having your heart broken. Every day. Advisors flew in from around the country—testing and pushing us in conflicting directions. The ebb and flow of creativity was crushing.

Thinking Wrong
Project M VARIOUS LOCATIONS

FOUNDER John Bielenberg
PARTICIPANTS (SO FAR) Andre Andreev, Nuzi Barkatally, Ben Barry, Tim Belonax, Bonnie Berry, John Bogan, Rachel Cellinese, Dan Covert, John Custer, Lucia Dinh, Charlotte Graves, Christian Helms, Cassie Hester, Bryce Howitson, Brian W. Jones, Jim Lasser, Dana Malas, Katy McCauley, Serah Mead, Satoru Nihei, Preston Noon, Jillian Perez, Kate Powers, Laura Prelle, Anne Marie Purdy, Arvi Raquel-Santos, Ellen Sitkin, Wendy Smith, Kodiak Starr, Dana Steffe, David Stychno, Sagarika Sundaram, Nic Taylor, Nate Turner, Charlotte X

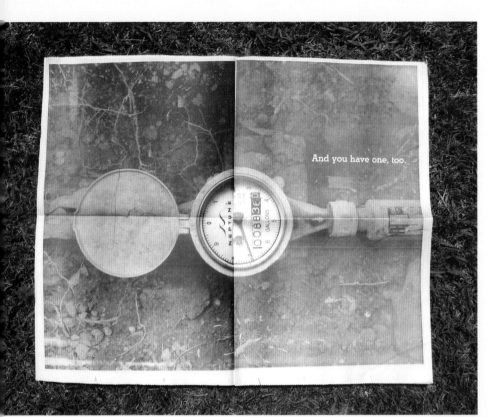

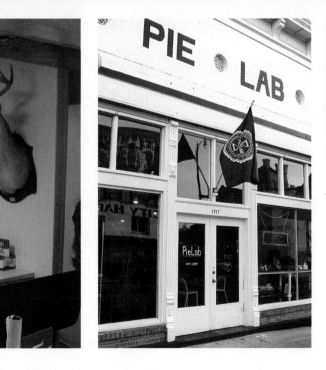

"This has to be *epic*," John would say. Directions like these froze us in our tracks. At times, we were as quizzical as Kubrick's apes gazing in wonder at the black obelisk of our task. John's *Think Wrong* exercises (like ideation through random word selection or massive "Renga" sculptures) attempted to break our prescribed thought patterns and illuminate alternate possibilities. Trusting in a different methodology is challenging, especially when results from the new way are unknown and the old way is so…predictable. But we learned to believe in the process and in the process, ourselves. That's about as well as I can describe my month in Alabama.

So what is Project M? Is it just a bunch of naive "design missionaries" trying to save the world? Or is it the next big design movement—one focused on producing less, saying more, and creating action? To find out, you'll have to experience it for yourself. Go to www.projectmlab.com.

ADVISORS Sean Adams, Erik Adigard, Bob Aufuldish, Rich Binell, Kim Blanchette, Adam Brodsley, Jeff Caldwell, Michael Carabetta, Art Chantry, Brian Collins, Erik Cox, Marc Diamond MD, Nilus De Matran, Karen Fiss, Greg Galle, Steff Geissbuhler, Bill Grant, Eric Heiman, Jamie Koval, Bruce Lindsey, Michael Mabry, Jim McNulty, Jennifer Morla, Victor John Penner, Sam Perry, Lana Rigsby, Laurie Rosenwald, Greg Samata, Stefan Sagmeister, Thomas Sevcik, Christopher Simmons, Rick Valicenti, Michael Vanderbyl, James Victore, Mike Weikert, Chris Williams, Ann Willoughby, Andrew Zolli

110
102
112
107
102
116
110
118
104
118
118

Welcome Back

BACK YOUR BLOCK '08 NxNE

EVERY DAY, ARBOR DAY

PLASTICS	SOURCE	118 ENERGY	DESTI
#1 PET			
#2 HDPE			
#3 PVC			
#4 LDPE			
#5 PP			
#6 PS			
#7 Other Plastics			
Biopolymers (non-GMO)			

PLASTICS

NDERSTANDING

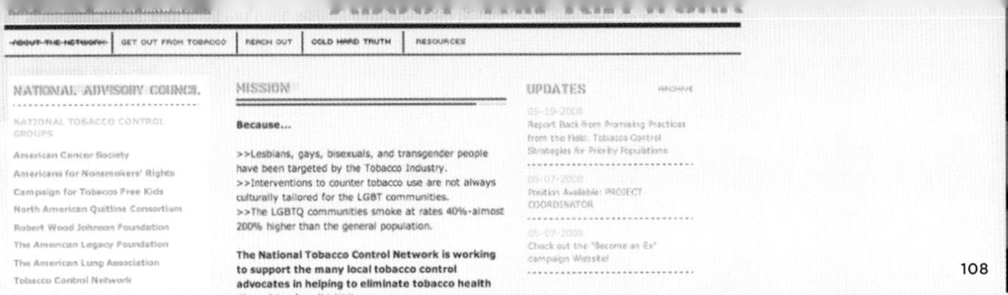

SUPPORTING

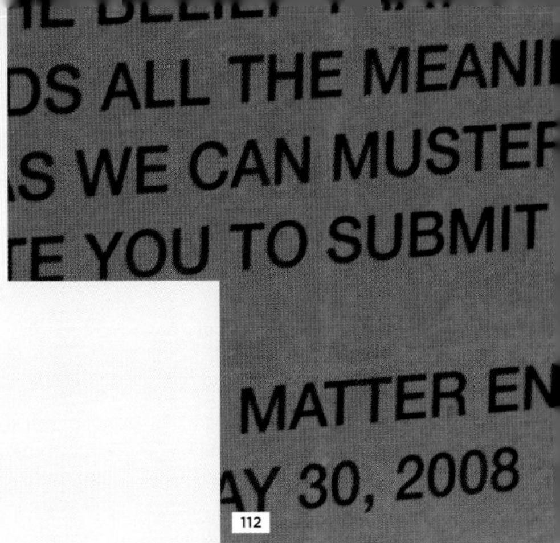

SEEKING

ORGANIZING

TEACHING

REACTING

CELEBRATING

How does design help spread the word, make people care and motivate them toward action? The following projects represent a range of approaches and perspectives on organization. They range from collaborative art projects that organize creative communities and transcend the proprietary studio model to organizing resources that unite people around communities of information. We look at the now ubiquitous silicon "awareness bracelet" (p.114) as a symbol of cause-based tribal unity, and how Nike is getting involved at the neighborhood level (p.114). We begin, though, with Aaris Sherin's assertion that all designers can be rock star ambassadors for good.

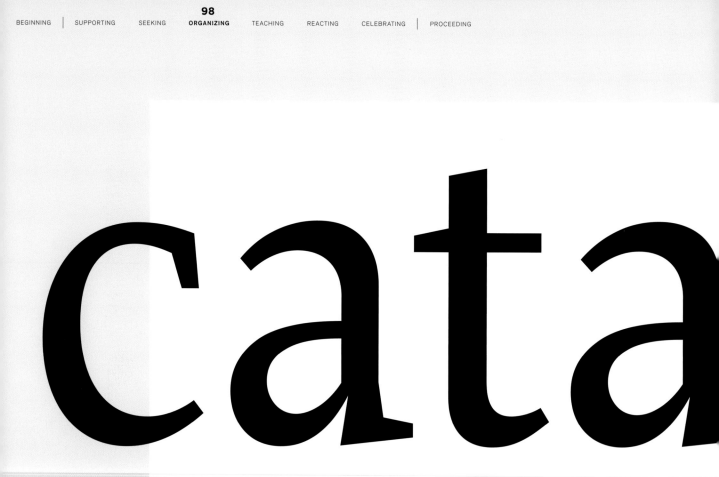

Aaris Sherin

Associate Professor of Graphic Design
St. John's University

lyst

What does it mean to design for good, and how can one be an agitator, an organizer and an agent of change? Good design is made by professionals who give a damn. Whether working alone or in collaboration with like-minded organizations, designers have the tools to be catalysts and make a positive impact at home, in their communities and around the world. Good design starts with doing what we do best and being flexible enough to adapt to a range of communication modes and outcomes.

Working alone is often attractive for practical reasons and because of the personal glory that is associated with a few "rock star" design personalities. However, a growing number of designers and sustainability experts believe that designers can be most effective when working collaboratively. The good news is that what collaboration and partnerships lack in glitz and glamour they make up for with job satisfaction and effectiveness.

First-year design students are often asked what it is that they will produce when they finish school. That list can become dizzyingly long. A graphic designer may spend a career mastering the intricacies of user-interface design, or she might create environmental graphics and signage for a museum one week and layout an annual report the next. Similarly, the ways that designers can help organize and generate opportunities for participation among audiences and consumers is as diverse as the output that we make. While we strive to do more, we should stay grounded and give ourselves credit for what we do best. Designers should design. Whether we build better experiences for viewers or develop sites to help citizens organize and campaign for change, we have an opportunity to align ourselves with causes that we believe in. The results are rewarding, stimulating and can add a bit of excitement to the day-to-day design experience.

Thinking in terms of scale can be paralyzing and even activists can get discouraged by how much there is to do. Fortunately, small steps are just as important as large initiatives. Mentoring a student from an underprivileged background or taking on an intern and helping him or her do values-based work can have far-reaching consequences. If every designer acted as a catalyst in some small way, the net gain would be tremendous. When we begin to think of motivating people toward action, we should start by making connections with like-minded individuals. Live by doing. It inspires others to do the same and there is lasting value in making design for good. There is no idea or job that is too small to start creating work that makes a positive impact.

As designers, most of us organize content every day. Organizing can mean hosting a discussion on ethical design, working with community organizations to interface with local populations or ordering and presenting information. In fact, making information clearer to an audience is one of the most overlooked areas of values-based design work. This type of "information design" is incredibly powerful and can be as simple as designing a website so that viewers can clearly understand a company's message or creating an information diagram about a health-related issue. In each case, presenting information in a way that helps the public make more informed decisions serves the audience and the larger community.

A clearer, better-designed world helps populations both rich and poor. How we get there is to make design part of every project, to make design integral to businesses, to non-governmental organizations and to service companies. As you work to create design for good, be an ambassador, be an advocate and remember that the little things that we already do may make the biggest difference. Motivating others starts with motivating oneself. So make design something personal and make it something that you believe in. In the end, becoming a catalyst works like the domino effect—one small action will lead to many others and to design for good.

Five ideas for becoming a rock-star designer for good:

1. Ask yourself, "What are my strengths?" Once identified, look for opportunities based on those attributes.

2. Ask yourself whether you can make values-based work where you are employed. If so, you might already be doing good. If not, consider whether fellow employees have ideas or beliefs in common—if so there might be opportunities to collaborate and work on ethical design projects.

3. Are there areas of your life—hobbies, faith, family or geography—that are particularly meaningful? If so, look for ways to interface with an organization or group that is part of your life already or one that is aligned with something that interests you. Put your skills to use whether they be design, communication or organization.

4. Keep doing what you do best. It might seem cheesy but a lot would be accomplished if we all "used the force" for good.

5. Avoid getting bogged down in the bigger questions or single-handedly trying to "save the world." First consider contributing locally, at work or in your community. Then, if you have the energy, rock on and tackle a global initiative.

Aaris Sherin is an associate professor of graphic design at St. John's University. She writes and lectures on the history of women in design, and social and environmental issues and their relationship to the discipline. She is author of the book, *SustainAble: A Handbook of Materials and Applications for Graphic Designers and Their Clients* and coauthor of *Forms, Folds, and Sizes: 2nd Edition.* Her writing has been featured in publications such as *PRINT* magazine*, STEP Inside Design, Novum* and *Design and Culture.*

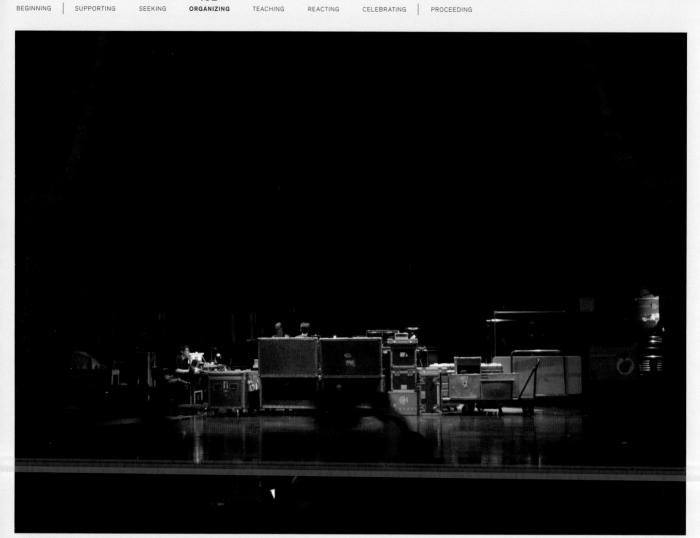

Compostmodern Identity 2004, 2006, 2008
Gary Williams and Robert Williams SAN FRANCISCO, CALIFORNIA

CLIENT AIGA San Francisco

WHY YOU SHOULD CARE However beautiful the strategy, you should occasionally
    look at the results. (Winston Churchill)

"Sustainability is a lot like teenage sex... everybody says they're doing it, but nobody's doing it well."

–Joel Makower

COMPOSTMODERN

COMPOSTMODERN IS AN INTERDISCIPLINARY DESIGN CONFERENCE dedicated to transforming products, industries and lives through sustainable design. Conceived in 2003 by AIGA San Francisco's chair for sustainability, Phil Hamlet, the biannual conference has grown to become a world-class event and a center for thought leadership around designing for environmental, cultural and financial sustainability. To help achieve and maintain this position, Hamlet and subsequent producers (respectively Jennifer Pattee, Amos Klausner, Gaby Brink, Don Savoie and Rahul Raj) have thoughtfully evolved the conference over the years. As sustainable design has become more popular—moving from a niche interest to a strategic necessity—the event has moved to progressively larger venues, resisted an effort to move the conference to New York, diversified its speaker lineup and expanded to include a second day. The conference website, designed by Addis Creson, has moved away from a strictly promotional platform to become a repository of inspirational presentations and practical resources.

Compostmodern is one part traditional conference—with high-profile speakers like Yves Behar, Valerie Casey, Bruce Mau and Alex Steffen offering inspiration from the stage—and one part experiment, culminating in an open format "unconference." At the unconference, attendees (or "participants," as their conference name tags read) create their own event by hosting workshops, breakout groups and plenary meetings in a series of impromptu, ad hoc sessions. What sounds like a messy process is surprisingly effective. Participants organize around their passions, often converting their shared enthusiasm into real action long after the conference's conclusion.

Multiply 20 designers by 50 cans of spray paint, divide by 5,000 posters and you get this:

THE WAY WE WORK

(TOGETHER)

SOUTHERN EXPOSURE GALLERY (SOEX) is a nonprofit organization dedicated to presenting diverse, innovative and accessible contemporary art. For their 30TH anniversary, SOEX conceived an ambitious exhibition titled *The Way We Work.* Celebrating its community-based roots and consciously acknowledging its collaborative working style, *The Way We Work* was comprised of seven collaborative projects, each involving a greater community to create and/or present the work. The goal was to explore dynamic and inventive ways for artists to share knowledge and produce original work through shared and open processes.

It was in this spirit that the design firms Mende Design and Volume Inc. chose to collaborate on the exhibition identity and invitation. Working together, they created an exhibition poster format that served as a kind of empty vessel which, they hoped, would later be filled by the public. The blank posters, united by repeated bands of split typography at their edges, were wheat pasted in fifteen locations around the city.

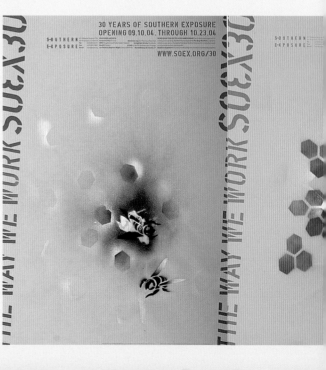

Announcements (in the form of cutout stencils) invited recipients to the show and also invited them to participate by filling those empty posters with their own creative interpretations of "work." To help jump-start that process, the duo used the promise of beer and pizza to lure about twenty of their designer friends to a outdoor work party. The group produced roughly 300 original posters, which were then seeded amongst their unadorned counterparts—a gesture of permission to encouragement others to add to the waiting canvases. Acting as compatriots rather than competitors, the two firms initiated and managed a multilevel collaboration balance faith and planning and enrolled rival designers, friends, students and ultimately the public at large.

The Way We Work
MendeDesign / Volume Inc. SAN FRANCISCO, CALIFORNIA

ART DIRECTORS Adam Brodsley, Eric Heiman, Jeremy Mende
DESIGNERS Adam Brodsley, Eric Heiman, Jeremy Mende, Amadeo DeSouza
CLIENT Southern Exposure

WHY YOU SHOULD CARE Design is a process that creates order out of chaos.
(Clement Mok)

English / Español / Polish

VIEW OUR PROGRAMS

WORKER CENTER
BUILDING BRIDGES PROJECT
FAITH LABOR SOLIDARITY

Arise Chicago brings the moral voice to workers' struggles

OUR MISSION

ARISE Chicago builds partnerships between FAITH communities and WORKERS to fight workplace injustice through EDUCATION and ORGANIZING and ADVOCATING for public policy CHANGES.

SUPPORT WORKERS' RIGHTS

DONATE NOW

GET INVOLVED

CONTACT US

WHO WE ARE

Arise Chicago, formerly Chicago Interfaith Committee on Worker Issues, was founded by Monsignor Jack Egan, Rabbi Robert Marx, United Methodist Bishop Jesse De Witt, and Kim Bobo in 1991. With knowledge that the basic tenets of all faith traditions support the rights of workers, Arise Chicago organizes the religious community to bring about just resolutions to workplace injustice.

When workers wish to form a union, they are often met with intimidation and harassment. Arise Chicago organizes religious leaders through its Faith and Labor Solidarity program to support workers seeking unionization.

Arise Chicago's Building Bridges Program, begun in 2000, prepares women and people of color for the building trades' (carpenters, electricians, plumbers, etc.) entrance exams into apprenticeship

NEWSLETTER

Download our latest newsletter here, or sign up below to receive them in the future.

email me the newsletter!   SIGN UP ➡

➡ VIEW NEWSLETTER ARCHIVE

IN THE NEWS

Clergy Join Quad City Die Casting's Protest Executive Director, Rev. C.J. Hawking

Arise Chicago Identity and Website
Firebelly Design CHICAGO, ILLINOIS

CREATIVE DIRECTOR Dawn Hancock   ART DIRECTOR Will Miller
DESIGNER Sage Brown   DEVELOPER Keith Norman
CLIENT Arise Chicago

WHY YOU SHOULD CARE   They've based their business on being good people.

CLEVELAND 614 W Superior Ave, Ste 1200 Cleveland OH 44113 • mtaphorn@ohiocitizen.org • 216-623-3952 CINCINNATI 2330 Victory Pkwy, Ste 305 Cincinnati OH 45206 • abaker@ohiocitizen.org • 513-221-2115 COLUMBUS 1200 Chambers Road, Ste 307 Columbus OH 43212 • swoodson@ohiocitizen.org • 614-487-8608

WWW.OHIOCITIZEN.ORG

◂◂ Arise Chicago

Firebelly Design's tagline, "Good design for good reason" is more than just a slogan. It's a mindset. In 2004, the six-person firm, under the leadership of owner/creative director Dawn Hancock, established a grant program—a yearlong commitment to give pro bono support to a nonprofit organization. In 2008, Chicago Interfaith Committee on Worker Issues was the beneficiary of that program. Firebelly initiated a complete brand overhaul, rebranding the organization under a new name (Arise Chicago) and developing a new mission statement and tagline. They also created a visual identity for the group, including a new logo system and website. The result is a dramatically more consistent and credible representation of the organization, and a substantially more useful and relevant website.

◂ Ohio Citizen Action

Posters will always have a place in grassroots activism and populist movements. Their visual impact, ease of production and distribution—and to some extent their legacy—all weigh in their favor. While not as deep an engagement as a fully articulated campaign or a complete brand overhaul, posters remain a relevant and resonant form of graphic communication. In this instance, Little Jacket's poster serves as a call to action to organize against local business polluters. As a public form of communication, it lets those same businesses know that the community is prepared to rally in their own defense.

Ohio Citizen Action

Little Jacket Inc. CLEVELAND, OHIO

ART DIRECTOR Ken Hejduk   DESIGNER Mikey Burton
CLIENT Ohio Citizen Action

WHY YOU SHOULD CARE   It kills two birds with one stone.

National LGBT Tobacco Control Network
Firebelly Design CHICAGO, ILLINOIS

ART DIRECTOR Dawn Hancock   DESIGNER Katie Yates   DEVELOPER Kara Brugman
CLIENT Fenway Community Health

WHY YOU SHOULD CARE   Big tobacco targets the LGBT community;
they are 200% more likely to smoke.

Superheroes Needed
Little Jacket Inc. PHILADELPHIA, PENNSYLVANIA

ART DIRECTOR Ken Hejduk   DESIGNERS Mikey Burton, Joey Parlett
CLIENT Make A Ripple

WHY YOU SHOULD CARE   Superheroes *are* needed.

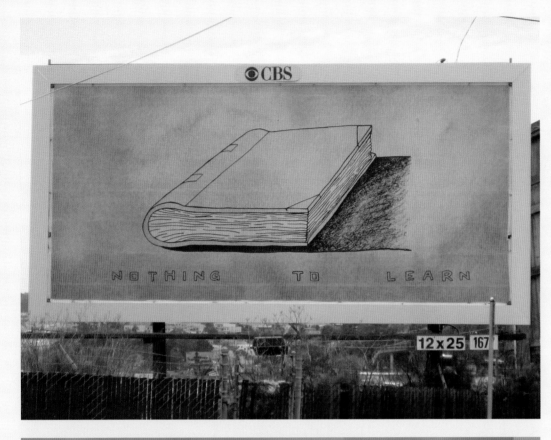

◄◄ LGBT Tobacco Control Network

Firebelly Design's owner/creative director Dawn Hancock lost her mother to lung cancer. Ever since, she—and by extension her studio—has been fiercely anti-tobacco. When they were approached with an opportunity to develop a website for a national campaign aimed at LGBT smokers, the project held special relevance. The site delivers information and resources that power a vast network of anti-tobacco groups across the country. It is heavy with graphics that lampoon the popular images and campaigns of major tobacco brands, but it also includes subtler cues which welcome and engage its lesbian, gay, bisexual and transgender audience.

◄◄ Superheroes Needed

Superheroes Needed is an environmental awareness campaign conceived by an 11-year-old girl. The campaign's goal is to help kids understand how to take positive action through simple everyday decisions, and effect change through their influence on friends and family. The campaign logo is playful and fun, without being overtly kidlike or falling back on condescending clichés. Because 11-year-olds don't have a lot of money, Little Jacket offered their services pro bono.

◄ Peace Billboards

The concept behind this project is simple—organize ten artists from ten different countries and ask each to create a billboard-size work imagining peace. Artist Richard Kamler initiated the project. His son Josh, a designer at Language in Common (p.78), and collaborator Jeff Caldwell of The Vega Project, collaborated on a website to promote and document the citywide public art installation.

Peace Billboards
Vega Project SAN FRANCISCO, CALIFORNIA

DESIGNERS Jeff Caldwell, Josh Kamler, Richard Kamler
ARTISTS Betty Nobue Kano, Clinton Fein, Igor Yusev, Jamyong Singye, Rafael Trelles, Richard Kamler, Taraneh Hemami, Tonel, Uzi Broshi, Victor Cartagena
CLIENT Richard Kamler

WHY YOU SHOULD CARE The first step to achieving peace is to imagine it.

Back Your Block

Digital Pond SAN FRANCISCO, CALIFORNIA

DESIGNER Michelle Brook   CLIENT Nike

WHY YOU SHOULD CARE   Corporations are shades of grey.

◄◄ Back Your Block

When you think of companies with a reputation for working toward the greater good, chances are Nike doesn't spring to mind. The company is hoping to change that perception with its Back Your Block program. Back Your Block is a national grant-making program that has so far awarded more than half a million dollars in support of 200+ local sports organizations. Designer Michelle Brook created the logo for the ambitious venture, along with a host of collateral including bags, banners, shirts window displays, posters, awards, email blasts and a website. The sheer force of Nike's presence – coupled with the avalanche of desirable branded material – brings new energy and renewed enthusiasm to the underserved communities where many of its grants were awarded.

◄ SF Culture Bus

The Culture Bus was an experiment that organized several of San Francisco's top cultural institutions in collaboration with the city's Municipal Transit Agency (MUNI). The special route linked Golden Gate Park's de Young Museum and California Academy of Sciences (pp.28–31) with SFMOMA, The Contemporary Jewish Museum, Yerba Buena Center for the Arts (p.190) and the Asian Art Museum. The route was served by a fleet of five zero-emissions vehicles sporting clever Pentagram-designed CB monograms against a distinctive yellow livery. Sadly, the pilot program lasted only a year. City deficits limited outreach efforts resulting in poor local ridership and confused tourists – proof that design alone (even really great design) can't bring success on its own.

SF Culture Bus

Pentagram SAN FRANCISCO, CALIFORNIA

ART DIRECTOR Kit Hinrichs DESIGNER Maurice Woods
CLIENT SF Culture Bus Project

WHY YOU SHOULD CARE Design creates culture. Culture shapes values. Values determine the future. (Robert L. Peters)

Ideas That Matter ▶

In 2000, the paper company Sappi launched Ideas That Matter, a grant-making program that funds creative professionals who want to contribute their talents to the greater good. In the ten years since, it has awarded $10 million in design grants. Ideas That Matter provided the initial backing that launched many of the design profession's enduring cause-based programs, including Joey's Corner (p.42), AIGA SF's Inneract Project, and Emily Pilloton's Design Revolution Roadshow (p.76). Grants have also funded projects for a variety of other initiatives, including projects for Amnesty International, The Designer's Accord, Planned Parenthood and others. Grant proposals are reviewed annually by a panel of judges, most of whom are practicing designers. Weymouth Design supports the program with a range of creative services, including the design of the annual call for entries, web design, photography and even the nomination of judges.

1% User's Guide ▶▶

The 1% is a program designed to connect nonprofit organizations in need of design assistance with architects willing to donate their expertise. The program was conceived by Public Architecture and launched in 2005, assisted by a grant from the National Endowment for the Arts. To help launch and facilitate the program, MendeDesign wrote and designed two booklets—one for architects and one for the nonprofits. The two books meet in the middle, joined by a common spine—a metaphor for the values shared by each of the two partnering entities. In essence, the publication introduces each group to the other so they may forge a partnership based on mutual trust, respect and understanding. The project was underwritten by Sappi's Ideas That Matter grant (see above). In its first 12 months of publication, The 1% User's Guide helped secure commitments from more than 150 firms and 70 nonprofits.

Sappi Ideas that Matter: Call for Entries 2008 & 2009

Weymouth Design SAN FRANCISCO, CALIFORNIA

ART DIRECTOR Rob Kellerman, Arvi Raquel-Santos
DESIGNER Arvi Raquel-Santos PHOTOGRAPHER Michael Weymouth
CLIENT Sappi Fine Paper

WHY YOU SHOULD CARE It enables good designers to do good work.

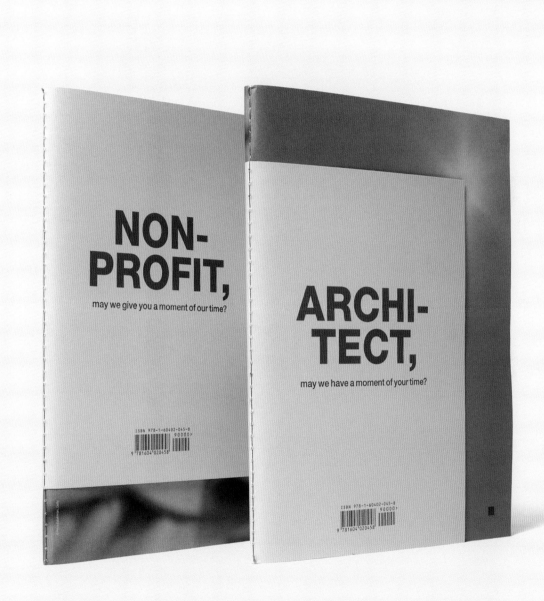

1% User's Guide
MendeDesign SAN FRANCISCO, CALIFORNIA

ART DIRECTOR Jeremy Mende
DESIGNERS Amadeo DeSouza, Steven Knodel, Diana Martinez, Jeremy Mende
CLIENT Public Architecture of San Francisco

WHY YOU SHOULD CARE   If every U.S. architect committed 1% of his or her time
                      to pro bono service, it would be the equivalent of a
                      2,500-person firm working full-time for public good.

AWARENESS BRACELETS

PRESUMABLY BASED ON THE CUSTOM of displaying a yellow ribbon in support of service personnel, the AIDS awareness ribbon—a red ribbon, looped and folded across itself—was created anonymously and copyright-free by the group Visual AIDS in 1991. It was first worn publicly by Jeremy Irons at that year's Tony Awards and quickly became the global symbol for the AIDS awareness movement. It also became an almost obligatory fashion statement among celebrities, spawning countless other cause-related ribbons (pink for breast cancer, red and blue for Haiti relief, etc.). By their nature, though, the ribbons were only occasional accessories, affixed to lapels and dresses and best suited for formal events.

In 2004, the Lance Armstrong Foundation (p.186) introduced its now trademark LIVESTRONG wristband as a means of raising money for cancer research. Often referred to as an "awareness bracelet," the yellow band (so colored in reference to the leader jersey worn in the *Tour de France*) was the logical successor to the ubiquitous awareness ribbon.

In contrast to the ribbon, the LIVESTRONG bracelet is everyday wear, designed for anyone to wear. Made of durable silicone, it can be worn regardless of activity, equally at home with a T-shirt or under a French cuff. The bracelets were initially sold for one dollar apiece, with all proceeds going to benefit cancer research. The low-cost, discrete but distinctive design coupled with Lance Armstrong's inspiring personal story and unparalleled athletic talent helped to popularize the accessory—first with cyclists and athletes and then with the public at large. Armstrong's February 2005 appearance on Oprah skyrocketed sales, which reached 32 million shortly after the episode aired.

Like the AIDS ribbon, the silicone bracelet format was soon co-opted by dozens of other nonprofit organizations and others hoping to promote a cause or point of view. The campaign Make Poverty History was the first to follow Armstrong's lead with their still-popular "white band." Today there are countless of variations on the theme—ranging from Katrina relief to patriotism to saving the frogs. Increasingly, the bands symbolize support or solidarity with ideals, not acknowledgment of a charitable contribution, as was originally the case. The band's ability to publicly signify affinity has made them more of an identity accessory than anything.

In a sign the cause bracelet had overstepped its tipping point, in 2008 comedian Stephen Colbert launched his satirical WRISTSTRONG campaign. Ostensibly promoting "wrist awareness," sales of the red silicone band have so far raised more than $250,000. Perhaps unknowingly closing the loop on the bracelet's evolutionary heritage, Colbert donates the proceeds to a veteran's organization called the Yellow Ribbon Fund.

Open for Business:
Opportunities in the Excelsior

Excelsior Business Attraction ▶

The Excelsior Action Group is a community organization formed to strengthen the business corridor of San Francisco's outlying Mission-Excelsior neighborhood. Their brochure highlights the many advantages of locating a business in the neighborhood (just as the designer Julio Martínez's family once did) and uses the familiar metaphor of a storefront "OPEN" sign as a recurring theme throughout. Although the brochure cites numerous bits of statistical, demographic and financial information in support of its cause, the designers wanted it to have a personal voice as well. To achieve this, they photographed the OPEN signs of local businesses in the district and credited each of them. It's a small touch, but one that invites the prospective business into an "open" and supportive community.

Excelsior Business Attraction
studio1500 SAN FRANCISCO, CALIFORNIA

DESIGNER Julio Martínez CLIENT Excelsior Action Group

WHY YOU SHOULD CARE   Good design is good business. (Thomas Watson, Jr.)

◄ SHCP Vision Book

To attract both students and parents to Sacred Heart Cathedral Preparatory (SHCP), San Francisco-based MINE™ designed a vision book and application that told their story from two perspectives: one from the school and one from the students themselves. To tell the students' stories, the designers organized 12 SHCP students and gave each a digital camera to document a day in their life at home and at school. Those photo essays became one half of a two-part book, each sharing a common spine. By allowing the students to share their personal experiences through their own (unedited) words and images, the design helped paint an honest and realistic picture of student life at the school. Most importantly, it spoke to prospective students in their own language and on their own terms—welcoming them into the SHCP community before they even arrived.

Sacred Heart Cathedral Preparatory Vision Book
MINE™ SAN FRANCISCO, CALIFORNIA

CREATIVE DIRECTOR Christopher Simmons
DESIGNERS Christopher Simmons, Tim Belonax, Oona Lyons
PHOTOGRAPHER Jennifer Sauer, SHCP Students
CLIENT Sacred Heart Cathedral Preparatory

WHY YOU SHOULD CARE People ignore design that ignores people. (Frank Chimero)

"It's important that you tie yourself to something you actually give a shit about."

BRIAN DOUGHERTY

BRIAN DOUGHERTY IS PRINCIPAL CREATIVE DIRECTOR at Celery Design Collaborative in Berkeley, California. He is the author of *Green Graphic Design*, a comprehensive guidebook for ecology-conscious designers, covering topics ranging from picking the right client to building green brands to the details of ecological production. A frequent lecturer on ecological design innovation, he also serves on the advisory board of the AIGA Center for Sustainable Design.

Brian Dougherty
Celery Design Collaborative BERKELEY, CALIFORNIA
Photo: Christopher Simmons

How did you get started with "green" design? Around 1995, I read Paul Hawken's book *The Ecology of Commerce*. Around that time, I also read Sim Vanderryn's book, *Ecological Design*. I kept being exposed to these ideas by architects and entrepreneurs like Hawken and Vanderryn and Alice Waters, and I realized that I wanted to do that stuff too. Even though they were all coming from different disciplines, they all involved integrating systems thinking into business. And so three of us got together and started Celery. Paul Hawken was actually one of our early clients. He gave us $200 to do his identity, but that pulled us into that world of sustainable design at a time when it was really just forming. For a while, we were the only design firm that was offering that.

Is it easier now that you're more established? Sustainable design is much less foreign to mainstream marketing and it's more familiar to more people in the business world, so in that sense it's easier. But there is still not a lot of institutional knowledge around most sustainable issues. If you walk in to a marketing meeting with any large client, they're going to be familiar with the idea of sustainable design, but they probably haven't done it. So it still can be a challenge, but it's also an effective point of differentiation for us.

Was differentiation part of your plan? Not at all. Systems thinking, ecology, sustainability, those are all interest areas for us. We built our business around those ideals and we worked with people who shared our values. It wasn't like we were going into Safeway and pitching them the idea that they should rebuild themselves as a sustainable grocery store. It was more like Elephant Pharmacy coming to us because they were trying to do a different kind of pharmacy, and they heard we were trying to do a different kind of design. We worked together with clients like that because we had something in common. Today, I think a lot of people see "green design" as a kind of market segment, but we've never looked at it that way.

It's more important that you tie yourself to something you actually give a shit about. If sustainability doesn't float your boat, don't do it. If you're really into underground music, you can become an amazing designer by immersing yourself in that world. If you're really into literature, you should be at 826 every day. What you'll find is, if you go deep enough, eventually you'll be the only designer in the room. You'll work with people who share your interests and the result will be a really fulfilling design career—that happens by pursuing your passions, not by chasing a market segment.

Is it harder to run a studio committed to sustainable practice? Does the additional research, effort and education it takes ever become a burden? It's no more burden than gravity. If you're from Earth and you go to Jupiter, gravity seems like a really big deal, but if you grew up on Jupiter, it doesn't seem bad at all. It's just what you know. So if I want to create a bottle made of 100% post consumer waste and I have to call seventy vendors until I find one who can do it for us, and that takes me 200 hours, I don't worry about how I'm going to bill for that, I just do it. I do it because I want to. It's not a burden any more than kerning is a burden. That's the way we approach sustainability—it's part of our craft.

New crossing markings differentiate this intersection
from others, and full color bike lanes help make the intersection of bicycle facilities apparent.

Trail signs alert riders that that they have reached
the trail, and explain to drivers why the intersection is
marked differently than they are used to.

The simplified bicycle symbol can be used for new
bicycle facilities as the Seattle Bicycling Master Plan is
carried out.

138

130 132

MUNITY RESOURCES

142

EARTHQUA

EXPLORATION

SOUTHE

137

Sutton House Inc.

128

9∂

139

RECYCLE

122

132

130

124

SOFTY! · BE A SOFTY! · BE A SOFTY! · BE A SOFTY! · BE A SOFTY! · BE A SOFTY! · BE A SOFTY!

RESO
LUTION

SUPPORTING

SEEKING

ORGANIZING

TEACHING

REACTING

CELEBRATING

Young people—especially students—are generally the most motivated group when it comes to social change. They have more physical energy to invest than at any other point in their lives and typically more passion and optimism to sustain that investment. They also have the least to lose and the most to gain from any outcome. So how are today's student designers being educated about their future roles as designer/citizens? How are design programs nurturing this passion and focusing this energy? Project examples from leading schools offer some clues, while California College of the Arts' Chair of Graphic Design Cinthia Wen offers her vision for a curriculum based on self-awareness and action.

F.A.R.M. ▶

Designer/educator Robynn Waxman describes her graduate thesis
as "slow protest." Like the Slow
Food movement, it is focused on
action and change, but takes a more
thoughtful, longer-term approach
than a typical protest. Waxman
was interested in exploring ways of
engaging millennial youth in reclaim-
ing neglected, overrun or contaminated public space. She used
Hooper Street—a run-down street
just north of her campus—as a test
case. Though she initially wanted
to attract a critical mass of students
to demand change, she soon realized that is not the millennial way. "I
wanted a mob," she says, "but they
delivered a group. I wanted them to
be agitated, but instead they got to
work, too busy to feel rage." Through
a year-long process of re-evaluating
her community outlook, Waxman
gained insight via message boards,
interviews, public meetings and
hands-on collaborations. She developed a plan to turn the neglected
street into a community farm. With
her collaborators, she developed
compost and planting zones, rain
sities that quickly transformed the
overlooked and decrepit street into
a center of action and optimism. She
documented the entire process in
tabloid newspaper and has since
rolled out a second F.A.R.M. project
in the state capitol.

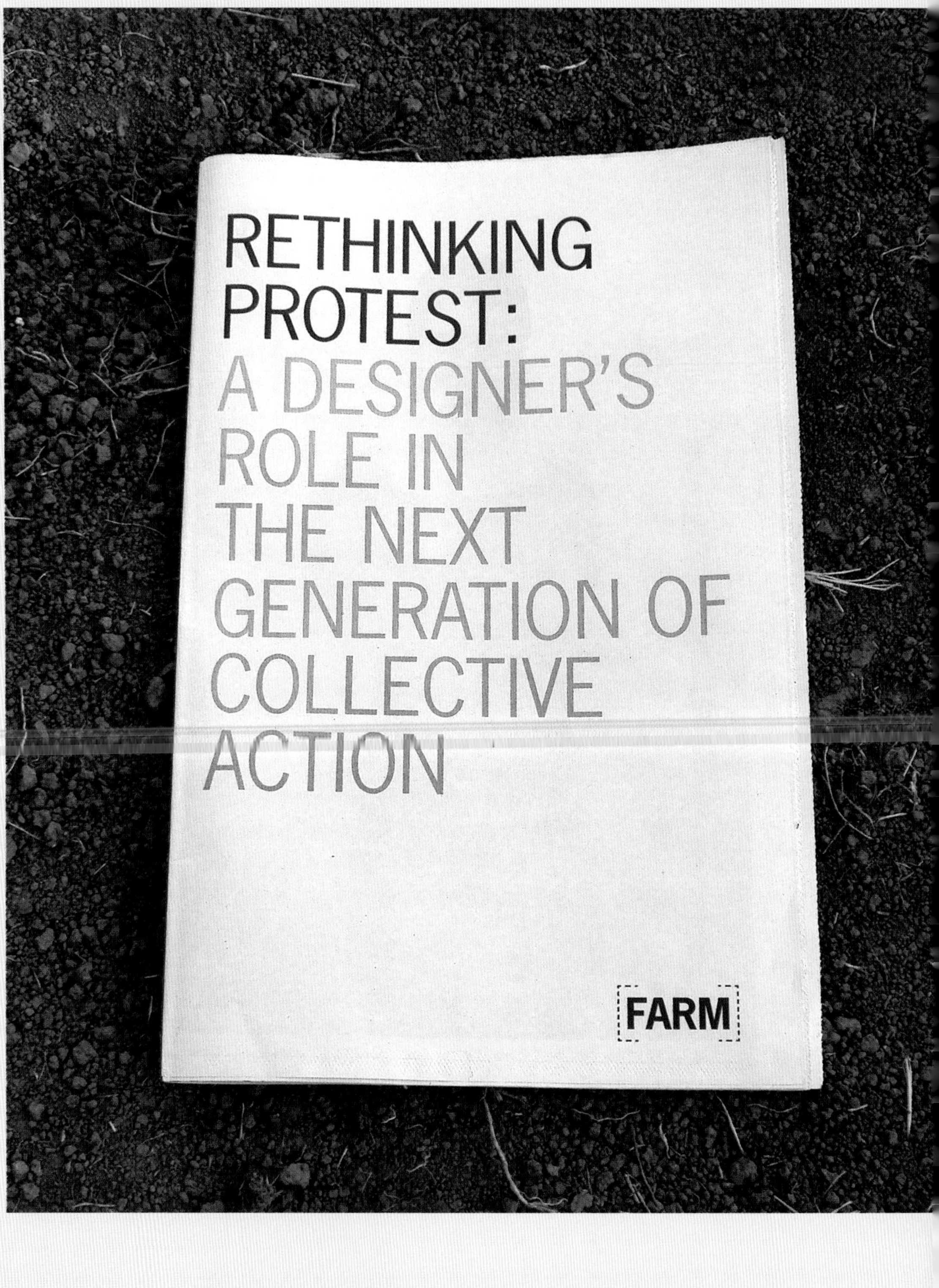

RETHINKING PROTEST: A DESIGNER'S ROLE IN THE NEXT GENERATION OF COLLECTIVE ACTION

FARM

21.

SATURDAY
MARCH 28, 2009
50+ STUDENTS, STAFF
& COMMUNITY MEMBERS
GATHERED TO BUILD A
SIXTY-SIX FOOT LONG
FARM ON A TOXIC STRIP
OF LAND. WE BEGAN AT
EIGHT AM ON HOOPER
STREET, THE NEGLECTED
SIDESTREET THAT BISECTS
THE CALIFORNIA COLLEGE
OF THE ARTS CAMPUS IN
SAN FRANCISCO. THIS IS
OUR STORY.

A RELATIVELY OVERT REACTION
TO EVENTS OR SITUATIONS:
SOMETIMES IN FAVOR, THOUGH
MORE OFTEN OPPOSED.
PROTESTERS MAY ORGANIZE
A PROTEST AS A WAY OF PROACTIVELY
PUBLICLY AND FORCEFULLY
MAKING THEIR OPINIONS
HEARD IN AN ATTEMPT TO
INFLUENCE PUBLIC OPINION
OR GOVERNMENT POLICY, OR
MAY UNDERTAKE DIRECTION
ACTION TO ATTEMPT TO
DIRECTLY ENACT DESIRED
CHANGES THEMSELVES.

F.A.R.M. (Future Action Reclamation Mob)
California College of the Arts, Graduate Design SAN FRANCISCO, CALIFORNIA
INSTRUCTORS Dennis Crowe, Michael Vanderbyl DESIGNER Robyn Waxman

WHY YOU SHOULD CARE Design is a framework for change.

WHAT THE *#&! IS SOCIAL DESIGN

What The *#&! Is Social Design
Academy of Art University SAN FRANCISCO, CALIFORNIA

INSTRUCTOR Phil Hamlett, Michael Sainato, Michael Kilgore
DESIGNERS Ashley Ciecka, Michael Jeter

WHY YOU SHOULD CARE It's important to give a *#&!

◄ What the *#&! Is Social Design

What the *#&! Is Social Design was an exhibition created by two Academy of Art University MFA students to encourage designers to work toward the greater good. Part celebration and part inspiration, the installation featured profiles and case studies, as well as some historical context, tips, resources and collaborative work spaces. Perhaps most importantly, it brought together a diverse group of designers both old and young (mostly young) in a critical mass of passion and possibility. The ambitious project took a year to research, curate, design and build — eventually encompassing the school's entire 1,000 square-foot gallery. The exhibition was produced on a relatively modest budget of $7,000, much of which was underwritten by a Sappi Grant (p.112).

Mike Weikert believes design is bigger than the designer, and much more significant than a portfolio.

MIKE WEIKERT

MIKE WEIKERT IS DIRECTOR OF THE CENTER FOR DESIGN PRACTICE at the Maryland Institute College of Art (MICA) and was previously co-chair of the college's graphic design department. In addition to running his own design practice, Weikert Design, he is a partner of Piece Studio, a socially-focused design initiative, and serves as an advisor to Project M.

Mike Weikert
Center for Design Practice, Maryland Institute College of Art
BALTIMORE, MARYLAND

Photo: John Dean

What is the Center for Design Practice (CDP), and how does it relate to MICA overall? The CDP functions like an honors program within the institution, where select students from various disciplines work on funded projects with partner organizations (nonprofits, corporations, institutions, government agencies, etc.). It is open to students and faculty from multiple creative disciplines, including graphic design, environmental design, video, and interaction design interdisciplinary sculpture. Our goal is to engage students in the process of problem solving, ultimately using design to make a positive impact on society.

How did it begin? When I was co-chair of undergraduate graphic design at MICA, I had the opportunity to partner with the University of Maryland on a project/initiative called Biodiesel University (mobile education/production labs housed in converted buses that toured schools, universities and public events educating people about renewable energy and environmental stewardship). After the initial semester it became clear that to fully engage in these types of collaborations, we needed to break down the barriers between disciplines at MICA and to the outside world. MICA's leadership shared this vision, and the following semester, a small group of MICA students and faculty began developing what evolved into the Center for Design Practice.

Why a program dedicated to this kind of thinking? Why not just implement these principles curriculum-wide? MICA does embrace a socially responsible approach to design institutionally. That said, it is simpler logistically for students and faculty from different disciplines to work together if the projects are taken out of a specific discipline or department. The structure also allows us to identify interested students and faculty, and assemble appropriate teams for each project or initiative. Each project is funded by the partners through grant dollars or other sources outside of MICA.

How would you define "good design"? Design and the design process can contribute to positively impacting our world and creating positive change. The process, however, is more complex than simply designing a brochure for a nonprofit. It involves problem identification, targeting objectives and audiences, immersion into research, implementation of design thinking and strategy, and an overall collaborative, multi-disciplinary approach to problem solving. This approach to design should not be thought of as charity, aid, or volunteerism, but a significant contribution that plays an important role in local, national, and global well-being.

What's the most important thing for design students to learn today? The understanding that the value and role of design is much bigger than the designer or individual, and more significant than a portfolio. The goal is to translate ideas and information into tangible outcomes with the potential to change behaviors and make a positive impact on society. With this comes the realization that we are not only learning about design process, but about major issues facing our communities.

What is the least important? I think there is significance and value in all knowledge. The key is how we choose to apply it.

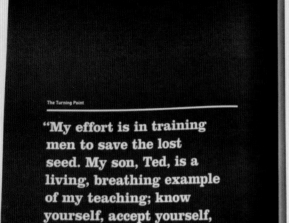

The Turning Point

"My effort is in training men to save the lost seed. My son, Ted, is a living, breathing example of my teaching; know yourself, accept yourself, develop yourself to be able to give yourself."

Dr. Stafford B. Sutton Sr.

Dr. Stafford B. Sutton Sr.
Ted's Father and Pastor of the Maryland Church of God in Christ and Columbia Church of God in Christ

Sutton House
Maryland Institute College of Art BALTIMORE, MARYLAND

INSTRUCTOR Bernard Canniffe
DESIGNERS Bryan McDonough, Alex Pines, Eve Darmon, Sarah Gehring, Jaehee Kim, Katie Park, Jon Sauermilch, Celia Sozet, Lisa Weiss
CLIENT Ted Sutton (Sutton House)

WHY YOU SHOULD CARE Design doesn't isolate itself from problems.

CREATING
HEALTHY HOMES:
Eliminating Lead Hazards in Baltimore

EFFECTS OF
LEAD

CLEANING AND
PREVENTION

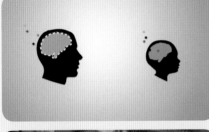

Dr. Tomás Guilarte
ENVIRONMENTAL
HEALTH SCIENTIST
JOHNS HOPKINS UNIVERSITY

20:44

40

30

20

◀◀ Sutton House

MICA instructor Bernard Canniffe created a class to encourage his students to connect with their counterparts in inner-city Baltimore. The open-structured, student-led class (supervised by Caniffe) partnered with Sutton House, a community organization founded by former gang member Ted Sutton. Sutton House offers mentorship, education and housing assistance to at-risk youth. Working directly with Sutton, the youth he serves (many of whom were active gang members at the time), and a budget of $1,000, the team developed a publication to increase the organization's visibility. The tabloid-format brochure highlights Sutton's inspirational story of redemption—exposing his past but ultimately looking toward the future. Soon after its publication, Sutton was asked by the city to share his experiences with Baltimore schools. Today, Sutton House continues to thrive and provide indispensable services; the nine students from MICA have likewise been transformed by the experience.

◀ Healthy Homes

MICA's Center for Design Practice (p.126) produced this eight-minute film for the Baltimore City Health Department. Its purpose was to educate local residents about the dangers of lead contamination. Consistent with the center's best practices, the student design team did field research by visiting Baltimore area homes where children had been tested and diagnosed with lead in their blood—a condition that can damage the brain and nervous system. This firsthand contact helped the students gain empathy for their audience and become personally invested in the project.

Healthy Homes (video)
MICA: Center for Design Practice BALTIMORE, MARYLAND

INSTRUCTORS Mike Weikert, Ryan Clifford, Allen Moore
DESIGNERS Colin Ford, Jillian Erhardt, Ryan LeCluyse, Matt Davies, Scott Lowe, Ian Scott, Christina Neston CLIENT Baltimore City Health Department

WHY YOU SHOULD CARE Good design begins with empathy.

HERO ▶

The Maryland Institute College of Art (MICA)'s Center for Design Practice is a collaborative outreach model that takes design beyond the abstract confines of the classroom and engages students and faculty with outside partners. One such partner was HERO – the Hale Empowerment and Revitalization Organization – an organization focused on helping residents of Hale County, Alabama find and maintain affordable housing. It's a tremendously effective program – once people know about it. To help make more people aware of just what HERO does, and to help potential beneficiaries understand how it could help them, a team of students and educators from the Center for Design Practice headed to Alabama. Lead by Center director Mike Weikert (p.126) who had previously worked with HERO via Project M, and supported by a $19,000 grant from Sappi, the team spent five days on the ground in Greensboro, Alabama, and a total of seven months researching and developing a campaign and support materials for the organization.

Global Water Gap ▶▶

In this installation by design student Nick Mendoza, each bottle represents a country. The volume of water in each bottle represents that nation's access to clean, safe water. Each is wrapped with a label detailing some essential water-related facts. The red line indicates the "water poverty line." That line represents the threshold of 50 liters per person per day that UNICEF and the World Health Organization calculate is needed for healthy living (20 liters is the minimum threshold for drinking and basic hygiene; the 50-liter figure also accounts for bathing and laundry). This information could have easily been presented as a table or graph, but by visualizing the data in a contextually relevant format it becomes easier to access, digest and remember.

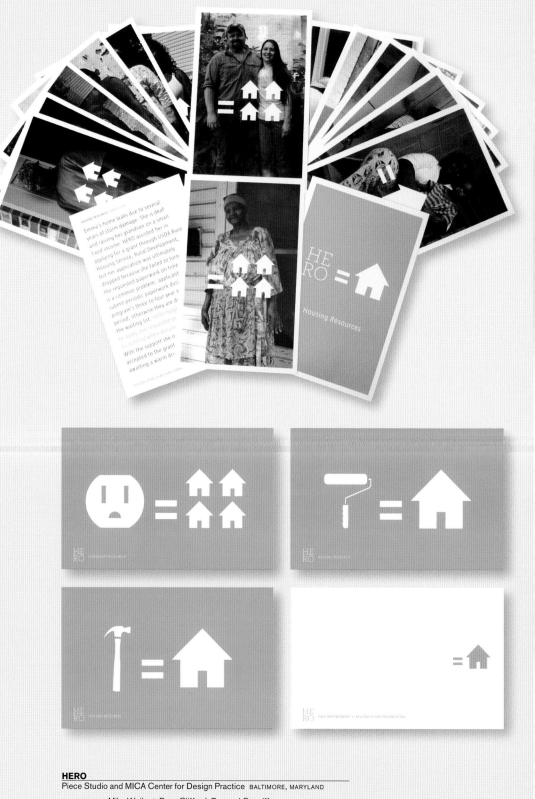

HERO

Piece Studio and MICA Center for Design Practice BALTIMORE, MARYLAND

INSTRUCTORS Mike Weikert, Ryan Clifford, Bernard Canniffe
LEAD DESIGNER Luke Williams DESIGNERS Hayley Griffin, Bryan McDonough,
Alex Pines WRITER Elizabeth Evitts Dickinson ADVISOR John Bielenberg
CLIENT Hale Empowerment and Revitalization Organization

WHY YOU SHOULD CARE   Design thinking requires design action.

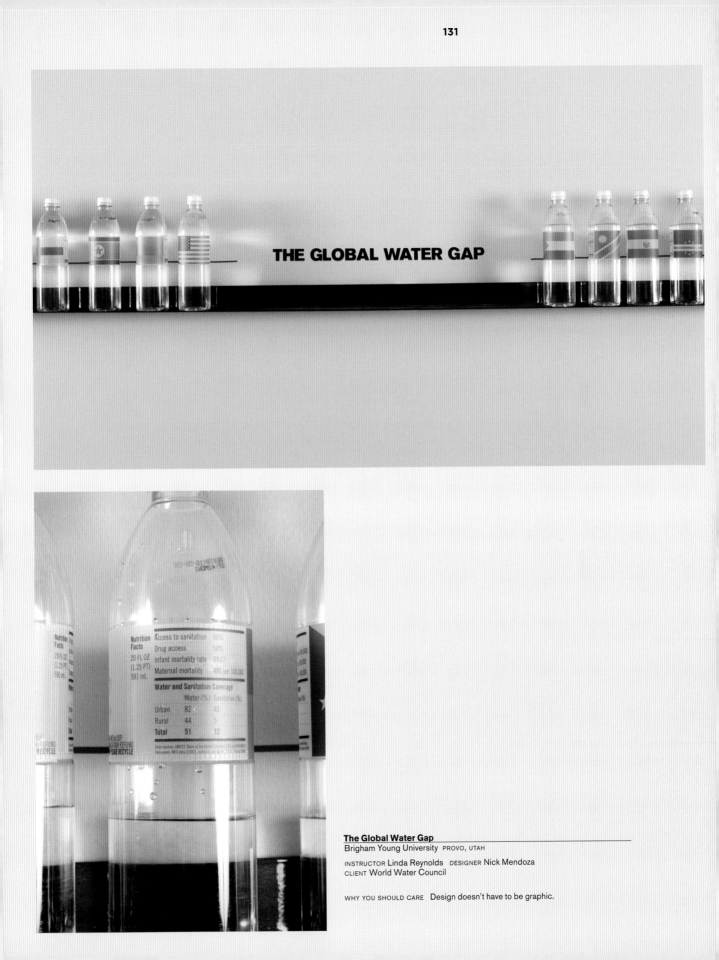

THE GLOBAL WATER GAP

The Global Water Gap
Brigham Young University PROVO, UTAH

INSTRUCTOR Linda Reynolds   DESIGNER Nick Mendoza
CLIENT World Water Council

WHY YOU SHOULD CARE   Design doesn't have to be graphic.

R3 Lab ▶

R3 stands for Rethink/Reimagine/Redesign. It is a collective response by students at the Academy of Art University, under the leadership of instructor Tom Sieu, to focus on designing better things and better experiences. It is an effort to transform the classroom into a socially-engaged think tank—and to place the issues of cultural, economic and environmental sustainability as the top priorities in a student's design process. Though in many ways still in its fledgling stage, the curricular experiment has already garnered the attention of AIGA, Adobe, The Designers Accord and Charlie Rose.

Green Guide ▶▶

The green guide is designed and written by University of Florida students, and attempts to dismiss the myths and stigma associated with living a green lifestyle. The guide seeks to maximize its relevance by including tips, statistics, facts, information and a pull-out poster-sized bike map opposite to the university. Simultaneously, it provides information and resources to underpin a long-term sustainable lifestyle. The student team determined that a printed document was the most effective and appropriate format for the publication. Conscious of the irony inherent in that strategy, the group researched alternative materials and methods to minimize waste, streamline production, and make the most efficient use of energy.

R3 Lab

Academy of Art University SAN FRANCISCO, CALIFORNIA

INSTRUCTOR Tom Sieu DESIGNERS Cristian Butcovich, Erik Carnes, Lauren Forbes, Judy Hsu, Andrew Johnson, Jeanette Karthaus, Emily Lemmer, Shani Lyons, Jup Tummanon, Rodrigo Zapata CLIENT R3 Lab

WHY YOU SHOULD CARE We can't solve problems by using the same thinking that created them. (Albert Einstein)

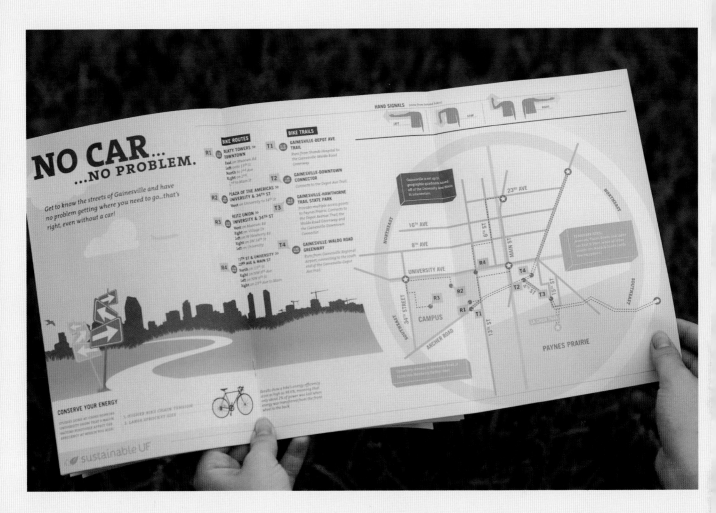

Green Guide Edition 3

University of Florida GAINESVILLE, FLORIDA

DESIGNERS Ariella Mostkoff and Morgan Slavens
CLIENTS Anna Prizzia and Dedee DeLongpré

WHY YOU SHOULD CARE   Change starts locally.

Kids Need Dads

School of Visual Arts NEW YORK, NEW YORK

INSTRUCTOR William Morrisey   DESIGNER Timothy Goodman

WHY YOU SHOULD CARE   It is fearless.

◀◀ Kids Need Dads

Children growing up in single-parent households are four times more likely to smoke, five times more likely to commit suicide, twenty times more likely to commit rape and thirty-two times more likely to become runaways. In most single-parent households it is the father who is absent. In light of this, designer Timothy Goodman—who grew up conscious of the absence of his own biological father—describes fatherlessness as "the most significant social issue facing America today." His eight-month project, Kids Need Dads, is a culmination of his own experiences and supplemental research. It is a comprehensive program made up of educational resources and public awareness pieces he wrote, designed and illustrated himself. Dependent on context, Goodman alternately used humor and sobering reality to deliver his critical message.

◀ Where does it go?

When the California College of the Arts (CCA) implemented its new waste-sorting program, students were initially confused about how to separate their trash. Recycling cardboard and cans is easy, but trickier items like pizza boxes, disposable forks and beverage cups caused some confusion (all three are compostable, by the way).To help clarify the issue, CCA's Director of Facilities and Operations Michael Welch enlisted the help of undergraduate design student Ellen Kieth and her graduate student collaborator Indhira Rojas. With the support of a micro-grant from the school, Kieth and Rojas designed a dramatic human-scale flowchart at the campus entrance. Using colored tape and black-and-white laser prints, the pair engaged both space and play to create a compelling information experience that quickly had their fellow students on board with the new program.

Where Does it Go?
California College of the Arts SAN FRANCISCO, CALIFORNIA

DESIGNERS Ellen Keith, Indhira Rojas

WHY YOU SHOULD CARE   Good design makes choices clear. (AIGA)

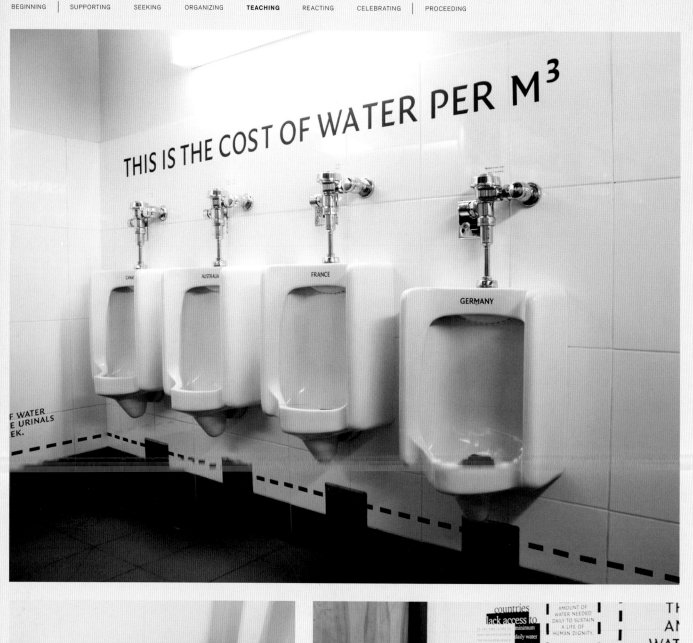

THIS IS THE COST OF WATER PER M³

CANADA   AUSTRALIA   FRANCE   GERMANY

F WATER
E URINALS
EK.

THIS IS THE AMOUNT OF WATER
FLUSHED THROUGH THESE URINALS
EACH SCHOOL WEEK.

countries
lack access to minimum
daily water
standards.

AMOUNT OF
WATER NEEDED
DAILY TO SUSTAIN
A LIFE OF
HUMAN DIGNITY.

TH
AM
WAT
EV

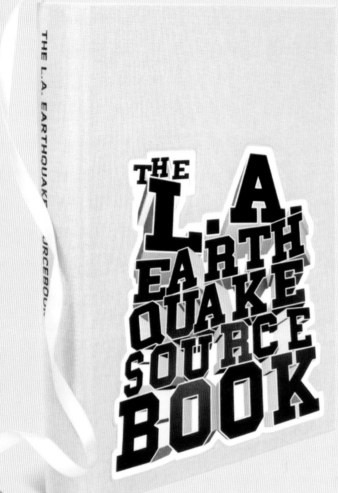

◀◀ **World Water Crisis**

To present research on the critical issue of clean water access – an issue which will soon dominate global economic, political and social discussions – Ross Milne didn't design a book or a poster or a blog, he designed an experience. Taking over an entire bathroom at Emily Carr University, Milne used the walls, stalls, sinks and even the urinals to effectively present both his data and his point of view. "I wanted to present the issue in an environment where water use is most prevalent," says Milne, "By creating this washroom installation, I brought the viewer face-to-face with the problem in a personal, non-intimidating way." The project makes intelligent use of the space – engaging its many surfaces, fixtures and overall volume.

◀ **LA Earthquake Sourcebook**

Art Center College of Design's *The LA Earthquake Sourcebook* was created to prepare Californians for the impending "Big One." Designer Stefan Sagmeister and his staff collaborated with Art Center students, who produced illustrations for the book. Self-described as "the coolest earthquake preparedness book ever published," the hefty guide lives up to its billing, making use of essays, graphic how-to guides and illustrative typography to deliver real facts and essential strategies for surviving the next big quake. The book was edited by David Ulin, book review editor for the *Los Angeles Times*, and includes an introductory essay by former FEMA Director James Lee Witt.

World Water Crisis
Emily Carr University VANCOUVER, CANADA

INSTRUCTOR Clément Vincent DESIGNER Ross Milne

WHY YOU SHOULD CARE The medium is the message.

LA Earthquake Sourcebook
Sagmeister, Inc. NEW YORK, NEW YORK

ART DIRECTOR Stefan Sagmeister DESIGNERS Richard The, Joe Shouldice, Mark Pernice ILLUSTRATOR Stephan Walter
CLIENT Art Center College of Design

WHY YOU SHOULD CARE It's not all doom and gloom.

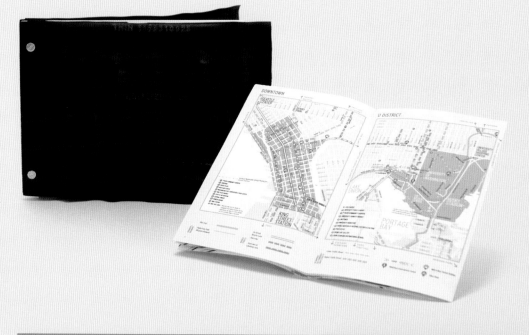

VeloCity ▶

University of Washington student Erin Williams wanted to change perceptions about alternative transportation—especially biking. Her approach was to attempt to shift the public perception of "normal" by distributing an alternate set of clear, attractive information. "The information put out by regulatory agencies and others has a huge influence over what the public sees as 'normal,'" she says, "and it's our perception of social norms that drive many of our decisions." Using reclaimed materials, she designed outdoor information kiosks to educate the public on the benefits of cycling, its impact, and provide community information. She also used reclaimed inner tubes and FSC-certified paper to create informational pocket guides to support those already cycling.

NonCents ▶

Besides having a great name, this exhibit by University of Washington students Simon Bond, Joey Flynn, Leonardo Hartono and Minh Vuol takes a critical look at a part of our daily life we take for granted: the penny. Consider this: Every penny produced generates 25 times its weight in waste and costs between 1.4¢ and 1.7¢ to produce. If four tenths of a cent doesn't sound like much, consider that in 2009, the U.S. Mint produced 2.3 billion cents. Do the math and you realize that it cost $920 million over face value just to mint the penny, producing about 1.2 million pounds of waste in the process. Those are pretty sobering numbers in support of a coin that has virtually no buying power. The NonCents exhibit advocated the elimination of the 1¢ coin, arguing that it is both economically and environmentally unsustainable. The team installed a pennies-only parking meter directly outside the gallery, and provided postcards that visitors could send to the Federal Reserve petitioning for the penny's elimination. More than half the exhibit was constructed solely from pennies, including a 5,000-cent copper carpet leading to the gallery entrance. When the exhibit closed, the students returned the pennies to the bank for a full refund.

VeloCity

University of Washington SEATTLE, WASHINGTON

INSTRUCTOR Kristine Matthews   DESIGNER Erin Williams

WHY YOU SHOULD CARE Designers turn data into information and information into messages of meaning. (Katherine McCoy)

Choose the reason why you think the penny should be removed from circulation.

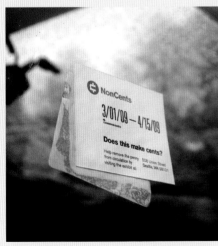

Put in your 3.4 cents.

NonCents
University of Washington SEATTLE, WASHINGTON

INSTRUCTOR Kristine Matthews
DESIGNERS Simon Bond, Joey Flynn, Leonardo Hartomo, Dana Vogt

WHY YOU SHOULD CARE   The U.S. loses almost $1 billion a year minting pennies.

Design Ignites Change ▶

Design Ignites Change is a program designed to inspire and encourage talented high school and college students to use creativity as a means of positively addressing social issues—ranging from diversity to homelessness to gun violence to hunger and water scarcity. With the aid of mentors, students are encouraged to develop real-world, sustainable and public projects, rather than simply exploring the issue on a hypothetical or solely academic level. The program is a partnership between Adobe Foundation and World Studio, a New York-based design and marketing agency that focuses on social change. The studio works with major corporate and civic clients, such as Wells Fargo, Whole Foods and others who connect their marketing goals with strategies for corporate responsibility. The same professional thinking and expertise that makes their corporate work so effective also informs their many social engagements. Design Ignites Change is the premier example of this, providing a rich and dynamic resource to a growing community citizen designers. By creating the context for creativity as an agent for change, and by promoting and celebrating the results of those engagements, the program is creating a compelling new reason for young people to aspire toward a career in the arts.

Design Ignites Change
Worldstudio NEW YORK, NEW YORK

CREATIVE DIRECTORS Mark Randall, Nina Mettler
DESIGNERS Randy Hunt, Ross Pike   CLIENT Worldstudio Foundation

WHY YOU SHOULD CARE   Art is a gift that changes the recipient. (Seth Godin)

◄ Cultural Roots

Since she emigrated to the United States from Iran, Samira Khoshnood's cultural heritage has found its way into her work in both subtle and overt ways. This class assignment explores the conflicting and complimentary aspects of her dual cultural identity. The poster, Cultural Roots, is intended to expose a western audience to the richness of Iranian visual culture in hopes of lifting the veil of misconception she says many have toward her homeland.

▼ GasTank

Designer/educator Mark Fox has long brought the ethos of political engagement to both his work and his teaching. This simple class assignment to design an agitprop poster is one such an example. Created in 2006 by then student Jon-Paul Kelly, the remarkably succinct "gas tank" symbol has been circulated the world over on sticker, posters and stencils. That the image has been so enduring is a testament to the resonance of design that has meaning—and meaning that has purpose. While other programs encourage students to redesign popular logos or create slick packaging comps for major brands (both of which are necessary pursuits) CCA has a tradition of encouraging a more personal and critical approach to design. In this example, that critical point of view is substantiated by its universal relevance.

Cultural Roots
University of Georgia ATHENS, GEORGIA

INSTRUCTOR Alex Murawski DESIGNER Samira Khoshnood

WHY YOU SHOULD CARE Design crosses borders.

GasTank
California College of the Arts SAN FRANCISCO, CALIFORNIA

INSTRUCTOR Mark Fox DESIGNER JP Kelly

WHY YOU SHOULD CARE It is both personal and universal.

The Last Resort ▶

Given the assignment to create an identity for a fictitious resort or spa, Serah Mead decided to take the concept three steps sideways. Rather than develop a lush luxury brand, she came up with an idea for a homeless shelter called The Last Resort. The "resort" had all the trappings of a luxury spa—custom shampoo bottles, towels and a beautiful brochure, but with one important twist. The artful handwriting that at first looks like a playful pattern is actually a vast directory of resources, tips and support agencies, making each item useful in both the short and long term.

When Mead looked for someone to model her blanket, she came across a man who called himself "Turtle," living in a makeshift shelter behind her school. He perked up when she told him about her project and asked, "Where is it?" Mead felt a flash of shame. "I felt sheepish telling him it wasn't real," she says, "But the blanket was real and so were all the resources I'd written on it and he really dug it." Turtle posed for her photo, then gave Mead the phone number of a man who could fix her boots.

Notion of Luxury ▶▶

For her senior thesis at the California College of the Arts (CCA), Janet Lai investigated the relative idea of luxury in the developed versus developing world. Her installation consisted of 119 handmade "Tiffany" bags, mounted on the wall. In each bag, she placed an artfully-wrapped envelope containing card of random denomination. Presentation attendees were offered a bag and invited to read its contents. The gift card might inform you, for example, that $20 buys one 3-D IMAX movie ticket, followed by a little information about movie-going habits. But flip the card over and you'll discover that the same $20 can also provide two weeks of safe emergency drinking water for a person in Haiti. Denominations ranged from $5 to $250,000, each drawing a the frivolity of our buying power into sharp and critical focus. In a final and conclusive gesture, Lai asked attendees to step back from her presentation, at which point they could see that the void left by the bags she had distributed spelled out a simple plea.

The Last Resort

California College of the Arts SAN FRANCISCO, CALIFORNIA

INSTRUCTOR Jennifer Morla   DESIGNER Serah Mead

WHY YOU SHOULD CARE   She let him keep the blanket.

$20

ONE AGRICULTURAL TOOL SET FOR A FAMILY TO USE FOR [

THE ADOPTION OF SUSTAINABLE AGRICULTURE THROUGH ORGANIC FARMING, M
LAND AND WATER AND NEW MARKETING STRATEGIES CAN HELP SEVERAL POOR PEA
INDIA COME OUT OF POVERTY AND HUNGER. IN A COUNTRY WHERE A WIDE MAJOR
EARN THEIR INCOMES FROM SMALL PLOT AGRICULTURE, IMPROVING FARM PRODU
HELPING TACKLE POVERTY.

The Notion of Luxury

California College of the Arts SAN FRANCISCO, CALIFORNIA

INSTRUCTORS Dennis Crowe, Michael Vanderbyl   DESIGNER Janet Lai

WHY YOU SHOULD CARE   It makes you think twice about your latté.

Cinthia Wen

Chair of Graphic Design
California College of the Arts

The world offers boundless resources, literally, at our fingertips. Information that used to require traveling, meetings, conversations or time in the library is now accessible by a click on the oval search button that has become an extension of ourselves. We have the option to earn a college degree, engage in fruitful discussions, share opinions or pontificate about our personal philosophies—all from the comfortable isolation of our ergonomic chairs. There is no denying the convenience of online chats, twitter, blogs and websites, but what does it mean in the larger context of a community?

What we choose to pursue and take responsibility for as "good" citizens depends so much on what we were, and are, exposed to every day. A friend who volunteers to serve meals on Thanksgiving at the local food bank presents me an option to consider how I might contribute to my community. A mentor who approaches me to create a course that engages design students to use their skills to promote the independence of women around the world encourages me to look deeper at gender issues. A 16-year-old boy in India who takes it upon himself to share what he learned from school each day to the rest of the children in his village makes me realize how lucky I have been and how much more I can do. A story of a Thai woman making usable goods out of garbage makes me conscious of my personal consumption and the waste that I create.

One response is to use our design skills to advocate for more responsible waste disposal. Through color-coded garbage cans, infographic installations, posters and detailed instructions we can inform a community about the differences between landfill, compost, and recyclable waste. Or we can do more. It is great to inform, but even greater to care about why we are doing this.

I was recently asked to define my vision for design education. Even now, this question is one that I cannot answer with certainty. The daunting responsibility of education is impossible to gauge and must be respected. A constantly changing world requires us to diligently evaluate and assess. What we as educators do, what we design as a curriculum, and the experience that we share with our students will necessarily shape the minds that then forge forward beyond us. Education requires the next generation to come first and personal ambition and ego to come second. It requires us to set a goal that we can and will do better, be smarter and care even more.

It is not about making goods for the sake of doing "good," it's about being connected to a world that beckons for our participation. As designers, we can take our ideas, problem-solving skills, aesthetics, need to communicate and entrepreneurial spirit—whatever we've got—and use it to encourage a better understanding of cultural, social and environmental needs. In this world where we are very willing to take, what are we willing to give?

I am fortunate to live and work in a part of the world that is rich in diversity and passionate about social and community engagement. It is my experience that designing for a cause or an issue brings people together. It takes the virtual community out of its remote solitude back into the physical world. I can wax poetically about social change, the power of one and the importance of human relationships, but ultimately there is no better method than to educate by example. Show students, "This is what I what I care about and this is what I do about it." Then ask, "What do you care about? What will you do?"

The umbrella of design is impressive. The access points where design impacts are marvelous. How each designer chooses to use her skills for "good" is unique. There is no right or wrong; all it takes is intention and motivation. As educators, we can inspire critical thinking, encourage each other to take on the responsibility in balancing the relationship between what designers do commercially and what designers can do socially to bring about a positive impact. In the classroom, we strive to engage in active rather than passive learning. We can use assignments as the premise to provide opportunities for students to engage, research and concern themselves with world issues. Exposing students to even a single social, environmental or political issue will instill an understanding that this is the domain of the designer. To educate is not only to ignite an idea but to also foster the courage to pursue that idea beyond the classroom.

Doing is worth more than a thousand words.

Cinthia Wen is the founder and creative director of NOON, a San Francisco design firm specializing in corporate branding and programs for arts, education, and cultural institutions. Her work has been featured in *HOW, Print, Graphis, Communication Arts*, as well as in numerous design titles and exhibitions. In addition to an enviable client roster, she designs a line of sustainable, earth-friendly products called simply, GOODS. Cinthia is an adjunct professor at California College of Arts, where she is also chair of the Graphic Design Program.

all
you
need

161

159

164

162

HED UP

RECIOUS -
sh Reborn as Art
Deb Ris
ashedup.us

162

162

156

155

YOUCAN

www.youcankingston.com 07941140771

162

154

stupid.

Love, Victore

150

162

LOVE
family joy
hope friends memories
anniversaries compassion
community
laughter
dancing
hug safety
kisses
early mornings fall
night light

161

I AM
CALIFORNIAN
EQUAL RIGHTS

151

160

Aftermath
In recognition and support of those impac...
Designed by Morgan Small for KeyLyt.l

161

162

161

152

SUPPORTING

SEEKING

ORGANIZING

TEACHING

REACTING

CELEBRATING

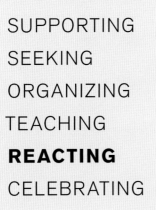

When the Berlin wall came down, I ran out of my house and screamed. I couldn't help myself. It was the most significant world event I had experienced and I felt compelled to share what I was feeling with as many others as possible. Screaming was all I could do. As designers, we are equipped to do more. Our abilities to communicate and to make—as well as our propensity to network—are tools that can be made to serve our visceral reaction to circumstances, events and situations. This section explores some of the ways in which design responds to the human condition. Whether the response is to a tragedy like Katrina or Haiti (p.159) or a local ballot proposition that represents a larger ideal (p.150, p.164), design can help generate cash, compassion or, as Alissa Walker writes, sometimes just catharsis.

153

good for the

Californian for Equal Rights ▶

Like many designers, Geoff Wagner had something to say about the passage of California's Proposition 8. But he didn't want to just say it to his friends and colleagues, he wanted everyone to know. So he made a protest sign. The designer in him couldn't help but make the sign typographically beautiful, and the people who saw it couldn't help but notice. A few started asking him if they could get it on a T-shirt. And then more. And so finally he printed up a run and sold them on the corner. They were gone in an hour. And so he made some more. He funded the project out of his own pockets and donated the proceeds to an organization fighting to repeal the new law. Wagner is still negotiating the nuances of product design, production and promotion, but meanwhile the shirts keep selling and his message keeps spreading.

29 Reasons to Vote ▶▶

Justin Ahrens, Creative Director at Rule29, describes 29 Reasons to Vote as "a conversation starter." Its content is consciously nonpartisan; the designers worked hard to either present both sides of an issue or select issues that transcend political ideologies. The self-initiated effort was originally intended as a studio promotion, but over the course of the project it became less and less about design and more and more about the election. "We just wanted people to get out and vote," says Ahrens, "regardless of their party affiliation." To that end, they gave the fruits of their month-long labor to anyone who promised both to vote and to hang the poster in a public place.

Please Save Us! Obama Gum ▶▶

Modern Dog designs a host of products for the novelty company Blue Q. Most are simple amusements or quirky, ironic "gift" items. All have a sense of humor. Some, though, also have an underlying cynicism or political message. Case in point: Obama Gum. It's hard to say whether it tastes more like hope or like change, but it's the packaging that seeks to make a difference here. "It reminds us of the mess Obama has to clean up," says designer Robynne Raye, a self-described liberal lefty, "I guess that's nothing I didn't already know, but it was fun to share that point of view on little packages."

Californian for Equal Rights

Swell Design   SAN FRANCISCO, CALIFORNIA

DESIGNER Geoff Wagner

WHY YOU SHOULD CARE   50% of doing good work is actually having it made.
(Paula Scher)

29 Reasons to Vote
Rule29 CHICAGO, ILLINOIS

ART DIRECTOR Justin Ahrens   DESIGNERS Justin Ahrens, Kerri Liu,
Kara Ayram, Tim Dammitz

WHY YOU SHOULD CARE   Complaining is silly. Act or forget. (Stefan Sagmeister)

Please Save Us! Obama Gum
Modern Dog SEATTLE, WASHINGTON

ART DIRECTOR Mitch Nash   DESIGNERS Robynne Raye, Robert Zwiebel
CLIENT BlueQ

WHY YOU SHOULD CARE   Even gum can have an opinion.

Republicans... EAT!
Studio of Brian Ponto BROOKLYN, NEW YORK

ART DIRECTORS Brian Ponto, José Chicas
DESIGNER Brian Ponto

WHY YOU SHOULD CARE You gotta fight for your right to party.

carpooling is bad for the economy

crime is good for the economy

self-esteem is bad for the economy

debt is good for the economy

nature is bad for the economy

obesity is good for the economy

◄◄ Republicans... EAT!

Using found MTA maps and free ink courtesy of the62.org, Brian Ponto created these anti-Republican National Committee posters in response to the RNC's New York City convention in 2004. Ponto objected to the RNC's tactics in suppressing free speech, which included designated "free speech zones" and outdoor containment cages for holding protesters. The maps were surreptitiously commingled with "regular" maps at kiosks in and around Penn Station, and distributed during a critical mass bike ride during the event.

◄ You are_____for the Economy

What is good for the economy isn't always good for people. Another of designer Brian Singer's self-initiated provocations, You are_____for the economy is an attempt to initiate dialogue about the real "economy" and the motivations that fuel it. Silk-screened chipboard posters and freely-distributed stickers act as topical grenades, launching shrapnel into an otherwise predictable public debate.

You are____for the Economy

Altitude SAN FRANCISCO, CALIFORNIA

DESIGNER Brian Singer   CLIENT Everyone

WHY YOU SHOULD CARE   Caring is good for the economy.

Advertisers think you're stupid ▶

James Victore sent me a roll of these stickers with no additional information or explanation. When I asked him to tell me a little more about the project, he said simply, "It's true." We'll leave it at that.

Advertisers think you're stupid.

Love, Victore

◄ **Sprint Reclaim Package**

Sprint sells a lot of phones and those phones require a lot of packaging. Or do they? In an effort to help minimize their unavoidable environmental impact, the company is experimenting with alternative materials in both their products and their packages. The Reclaim phone by Samsung, for instance, is made of a corn-based "bioplastic." About 60% of the phone is still traditional (petroleum-based) plastic, and the battery and other components contain some heavy metals so you can't just toss it on the compost bin when you upgrade, but it's a big step in the right direction. Even the charger is 12 times more energy efficient than the previous model. In addition to the device's eco-friendlier materials, the designers at Deutsch Design Works created a smaller, lighter box out of recycled materials to both protect and showcase the new product. A smaller footprint and lighter weight mean it's more efficient to ship, which saves fuel. When you consider the volume of product Sprint ships, those savings add up. If all that weren't enough, Sprint's headquarters is wind powered and the company donates $2 from every Reclaim phone sale to the Nature Conservancy.

Advertisers Think You're Stupid
James Victore Inc. BROOKLYN, NEW YORK

DESIGNER James Victore

WHY YOU SHOULD CARE Sometimes we need to be reminded.

Sprint Reclaim Package
Deutsch Design Works SAN FRANCISCO, CALIFORNIA

ART DIRECTOR Erika Krieger GRAPHIC DESIGNER Pauline Au
STRUCTURAL DESIGNER Karl Bakker CLIENT Sprint

WHY YOU SHOULD CARE Size matters.

Art You Can Xerox
MINE™ SAN FRANCISCO, CALIFORNIA

DESIGNER Christopher Simmons (after Shepard Fairey, after Mannie Garcia)
CLIENT Self-initiated

WHY YOU SHOULD CARE   Good designers copy; great designers steal.
(Pablo Picasso)

IN THE NAME OF ENSURING STABILITY AND HARMONY IN THE COUNTRY DURING THE 2008 OLYMPIC GAMES THE CHINESE GOVERNMENT CONTINUES TO DETAIN AND HARASS POLITICAL ACTIVISTS, JOURNALISTS, LAWYERS AND HUMAN RIGHTS WORKERS. **GET INVOLVED: WWW.AMNESTY.NL**

Beijing 2008
AMNESTY INTERNATIONAL

◄◄ Art You Can Xerox

Art You Can Xerox is a design provocation, generated in reaction to the Shepard Fairey / Associated Press legal battle over fair use. In that case, Fairey was alleged to have copied the image of Barack Obama for his iconic HOPE poster from a photograph by Mannie Garcia (a charge which he initially denied but later admitted). The title takes its inspiration from Hillary Clinton's quip that then senator Obama's policies represented not real change but "Change you can Xerox"—an apt metaphor for the degree of difference required before a thing is considered original. For this project, an original silk screen of Fairey's poster was purchased then photocopied—unaltered except for scale and the addition of Clinton's quote. The facsimile 8½" x 11" sheets were shrinkwrapped in reams of 500 to further comment on the commodification of appropriated imagery in art and design.

◄ Beijing 2008

Running up to the 2008 Olympic games in Beijing, many were skeptical of how compatible the Olympic image was with China's long record of human rights violations. Steven Spielberg famously withdrew as artistic director for the opening ceremonies, citing China's reluctance to use its economic influence in Sudan to end the crisis in Darfur. Several organizations and hundreds of individuals protested the choice of venue, both leading up to and at the games. Some demonstrated in the streets or signed petitions online, others turned to art or writing to express their disapproval. One such example was the Dutch agency I Don/t Buy It. Though not Amnesty International's official agency, when the designers learned of some of the abuses going on in China, they felt they "just had to design something." They offered the poster to Amnesty Netherlands, who were moved, but remained committed to the deeper engagement with their existing partner agency. Ultimately, the exercise may have been an act of catharsis but, the designers say, it's important to make the work that's in you—whether or not there is a client for it.

Beijing 2008
I Don/t Buy It NETHERLANDS

DESIGNERS Melanie Drent, Vos Broekema
CLIENT Amnesty Netherlands

WHY YOU SHOULD CARE   They didn't ask permission.

For every action there are infinite equal, unequal and opposing reactions. Here are a few.

FOUR REACTIONS

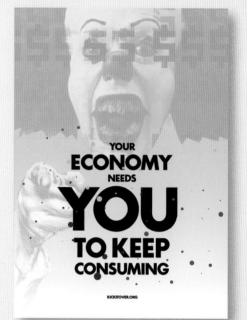

YOUR
ECONOMY
NEEDS
YOU
TO KEEP
CONSUMING

KICKITOVER.ORG

Make Some Noise

Design Anarchy is madness. Choose it only if you're certain all other options will corrode your integrity and consume your soul. Choose it only if you know yourself to be among those chosen few who hold Prometheus' holy fire in their hand. Because once you've set upon this path, you'll suffer for years and live like a stray, hungry dog. But you'll have the joy of breaking all the rules, of freely mixing art and politics and of pouring your beliefs and convictions into your work. Eventually, if you're really as brilliant as you think, you'll have a crack at pushing the boundaries of global culture with bold new forms and revolutionary new ways of being.

Kalle Lasn
Editor, *Adbusters* magazine

Adbusters Culture Jam
Adbusters VANCOUVER, CANADA

CREATIVE DIRECTOR Kalle Lasn DESIGNER Douglas Haddow
TYPOGRAPHY Pedro Inoue CLIENT *Adbusters* magazine

Make a Stink

Have you ever stepped in dog crap? It's disgusting, right? And no matter how much you clean your shoes, they're never quite the same afterwards. I found myself feeling the same way about a certain former president.

This experiential design solution quickly grew into a viral project that was shared around the world. Others began planting their own flags and posting photos to the site, which received millions of page views. Some people loved it, some hated it, but I think we can all agree that Brownie did a heck of a job.

If you feel strongly about a cause, put on your design-thinking cap and come up with a solution. Then hit the streets (or internet) with it, and see what happens. You might be surprised.

Brian Singer
Principal, Altitude

Make It Beautiful

In the face of large-scale humanitarian disasters, we naturally want to help but often we don't know what to do. As creatives, we have the ability to help by creating something beautiful and valuable. In turn that object can be used to raise funds and support humanitarian efforts. Designers are fortunate to be able to do what we love and earn a living at it. Banding together and using that talent to help others in need is one of the most positive ways we can react to a crisis. A good friend put it best, "As citizens of the world—let's forget graphic design, forget politics, forget nationality—it's our responsibility to help each other out."

Josh Higgins
Co-founder, Haiti Poster Project

Make a Difference

The empathy that provides designers with their intuitive and creative advantage can also ignite a compelling need to help others in a crisis. Often the instinctive response is to develop a campaign to bring attention to the problem. Crises, however, beg for unexpected solutions and the engagement of everyone as concerned and willing humans. Designers have special, less ephemeral contributions they can make: They use their ability to discover high concept, low-cost human-centered solutions; to facilitate creative responses and help others visualize them; and to serve as concerned citizens, not just designers. In the long run, these roles will place designers shoulder-to-shoulder with other concerned citizens, make a real difference, and help others to see designers as critical (maybe even heroic) contributors on the scene and in future challenges.

Ric Grefé
Executive Director, AIGA

Four More Years of This Sh*t!?
Altitude SAN FRANCISCO, CALIFORNIA

DESIGNER Brian Singer

Rebuild
Turnstyle SEATTLE, WASHINGTON

ART DIRECTORS Ben Graham, Steve Watson
DESIGNER Jason Gómez   CLIENT SoCal Fire Project

The _____ Poster Project ▶

In reaction to the devastation of hurricanes Katrina and Rita, Leif Steiner, creative director of the creative agency Moxie Sozo, organized the Hurricane Poster Project. The premise was simple—organize designers from around the world to help raise money for the victims. In all, more than 180 artists created limited-edition posters for the project. Their combined sales raised a little more than $50,000.

Two years later, wildfires scorched Southern California, claiming 15 lives, 1,500 homes and roughly half a million acres. Reacting to that disaster, San Diego-based creative director Josh Higgins (a contributor to the Hurricane Poster Project) decided to follow the same model and established the So-Cal Fire Poster Project. Higgins quickly enlisted the help of other expert partners, including the McRae Agency, who generated PR for the project, eventually landing Higgins on FOX News. Another friend, Robert Palmer, designed the website, and March 1 array provided the online storefront. Design blogs were quick to support the cause, and AIGA San Diego's Y-Conference helped rally the design community to the cause. In all, $21,000 was raised and donate to the Salvation Army's fire relief fund.

In 2010, three days after the Haiti Earthquake, Higgins and Steiner joined forces to create the Haiti Poster Project. With an experienced team in place and lessons learned from their previous two efforts, the two swiftly mobilized an ambitious international effort. In a show of overwhelming support, nearly 500 designers and artists contributed to the project, resulting in a gallery of thousands of limited edition posters. As of this writing, poster sales were generating $1,000 per week, benefitting Doctors without Borders.

Death Cab for Cutie Katrina Benefit poster

The Small Stakes OAKLAND, CALIFORNIA

DESIGNER Jason Munn   CLIENT Death Cab For Cutie

WHY YOU SHOULD CARE   They're making it easy to make a difference.

Aftermath
Morgan Smail SAN JOSE, CALIFORNIA

DESIGNER Morgan Smail PRINTER American Printing
CLIENT So-Cal Fire Poster Project

Roots Poster
Rule29 CHICAGO, ILLINOIS

ART DIRECTOR Justin Ahrens DESIGNERS Justin Ahrens,
Kerri Liu CLIENT So-Cal Fire Poster Project

Hope Spreads
The Office of Frank Chimero PORTLAND, OREGON

DESIGNER Frank Chimero
CLIENT SoCal Fire Poster Project

YOU CAN

You Can Kingston ▶

In London's Royal Borough of Kingston, the Cambridge Road Estate is a case study for health inequalities. To address this, a 12-week study was commissioned by the National Health Service (NHS) to discover the challenges to living a "happy" and "healthy" life in the government-subsidized community. As the design partner on the study, Think Public entered into an open engagement with the residents—conducting video interviews and public design workshops. Among their more innovative techniques was the creation of a text message service whereby residents could respond directly and individually to critical questions. Those questions were posed by guerilla-style murals in and around the community. At the conclusion of this co-design process, several key insights were realized. In response, the Royal Borough of Kingston, NHS Kingston and the Young Foundation (an underwriter of the study) created a new position: Social Entrepreneur in Residence. The post will steward the implementation of the study's recommendations and continue engaging the entrepreneurial talent of the community.

Washed Up Postcard Series ▼

Not unlike the Hogsmill River Antiques project (p.93), Washed Up is an exercise in creative reuse. The project is the work of designer Ann Shackman but is produced under the pseudonym Marina Deb Ris. Every day for the past twelve years, Shackman has taken it upon herself to clear trash off her neighborhood beach in Venice, California. Occasionally she's kept items that interested her—whether for color, meaning, form or sheer oddity. After amassing a sizeable collection of trash, Shackman realized she had a palette from which to design art pieces that spoke to both waste and ingenuity. Her work now provokes audiences in galleries and exhibitions in New York and the greater LA Area.

You Can Kingston

Thinkpublic LONDON, ENGLAND

ART DIRECTOR Paul Thurston   DESIGNERS Ella Britton, Alice Osborne
CLIENT Kingston NHS trust

WHY YOU SHOULD CARE   Good design is a good plan.

Washed Up Postcard Series

Anne Shackman Design LOS ANGELES, CALIFORNIA

DESIGNER Marina Deb Ris

WHY YOU SHOULD CARE   Graphic design is the design of highly disposable items; It all winds up in the garbage. (Karrie Jacobs)

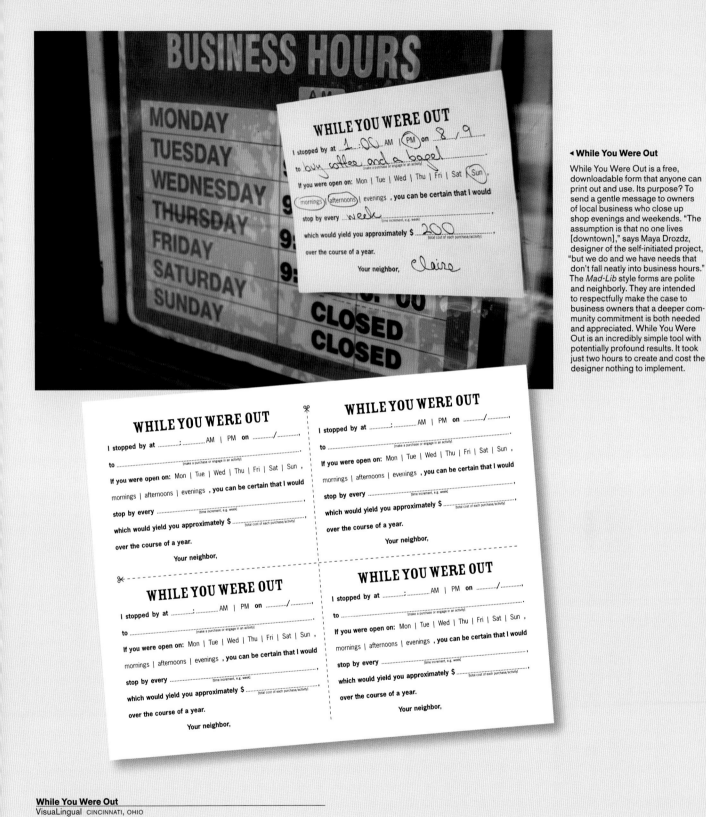

◄ While You Were Out

While You Were Out is a free, downloadable form that anyone can print out and use. Its purpose? To send a gentle message to owners of local business who close up shop evenings and weekends. "The assumption is that no one lives [downtown]," says Maya Drozdz, designer of the self-initiated project, "but we do and we have needs that don't fall neatly into business hours." The *Mad-Lib* style forms are polite and neighborly. They are intended to respectfully make the case to business owners that a deeper community commitment is both needed and appreciated. While You Were Out is an incredibly simple tool with potentially profound results. It took just two hours to create and cost the designer nothing to implement.

While You Were Out

VisuaLingual CINCINNATI, OHIO

DESIGNER Maya Drozdz

WHY YOU SHOULD CARE It doesn't overthink.

All you need is Love

John Lennon

stoph8te.org

POSTER BY MODERN DOG. PRINTING BY D+L.

Rethink Proposition 8

All You Need is Love

Modern Dog SEATTLE, WASHINGTON

DESIGNER Robynne Raye   CLIENT Stop H8te

WHY YOU SHOULD CARE   You shouldn't. Neither should the state.

◄◄ All You Need is Love

Proposition 8 was a highly contentious ballot initiative in California that successfully reversed a Supreme Court ruling legalizing same sex marriage. Despite efforts from activists, foundations, artists, celebrities, thousands of volunteers of all persuasions and $43 million in donations to defeat the proposition, Prop 8 passed in November 2008, effectively denying equal rights to same sex couples. Many artists and designers were motivated to fight against the constitutional amendment (the only one in state history to specifically limit individual rights). This poster by Modern Dog's Robynne Raye is a reasonable appeal to simply rethink the proposition. Inspired by the John Lennon lyric and channeling Sister Corita Kent (designer of the first love stamp), the poster is an elegant and beautiful gesture against the ugly backdrop of bigotry.

◄ Peace Is Not the Answer

"If you're for the war, or just hate peace, these posters are not for you," says designer Brian Singer of his series of anti-war posters. The posters—his design response to the Iraq and Afghan wars—were silk screened on recycled chipboard and wheat-pasted around the city. Singer also sent postcard-sized versions to friends and loved ones over the Christmas holiday with the message, "Wishing you war on earth this holiday season."

Peace Is Not the Answer

Altitude SAN FRANCISCO, CALIFORNIA

DESIGNER Brian Singer   CLIENT Everyone

WHY YOU SHOULD CARE   The essence of humor is truth.

grrr

Alissa Walker

Writer, Gelatobaby

People often ask me what makes a good design story. I'm sure they expect me to say something like using responsible materials. Or winning awards. But the best design stories have one perfect, crystallized moment: That time when the designer got mad. Like, really, totally pissed off.

That's because the best design solutions, in my opinion, come from anger. Anger can take any form: a deep-seated resentment, a roiling frustration, a slow-burning distaste, a quiet rage. You don't have to get all Michael Douglas in *Falling Down*. But if you're mad, that means you're passionate. That you're enthusiastic. That you're committed. I can see it in what you design. You'll probably have to explain that material you picked and how it's so sustainable you can eat it, but in a smart design project, without any description needed, I can clearly see the part of the process where you just. couldn't. take it. anymore. I can envision your idea enveloping your being, coloring you in this brilliant Amazing Hulk-green, your biceps bulging through tears in your shirt, as you push all of that pent-up, transformative energy through your oversized hands and into something good. Scary good. That's what the best design epitomizes. Anger forced into action.

It's natural for humans to bristle at the injustices we face in our daily lives, but designers are perhaps the most heavily burdened of all. Designers notice things. It's a curse that designers must carry with them for their entire lives. A pleasant walk through a nice-enough neighborhood suddenly becomes an assault to the senses because a designer starts to see all the things that are wrong. The sign is kerned poorly. The fence post is crooked. The window is broken. The parking meter is confusing. That person living on the street should be able to afford health care.

There's so much to be frustrated and incensed by these days in perpetual annovation. But designers are better-equipped to handle anger management than most. Designers, by nature, solve problems. They have the means by which to fabricate and implement a feasible solution. So while those poor environmental advocates stand outside the local grocery store in the blinding heat, trying to persuade enough shoppers to sign a petition, a designer can make something that actually functions, that works, that looks good, that makes a difference. Today.

Designers also excel in the ability to translate their anger into a vision that gets others on board. When a politician tries to rally a crowd, he'll build a bad PowerPoint and show it in a fluorescent-lit conference room that smells like stale coffee. A designer creates a poster, a campaign, a website—an attractive way to build buy-in. Using realistic visual renderings or abstracted symbols, designers can illustrate the future for a new audience: "This is what it will look like, this is what you will like about it." An idea, transformed by a designer, gets attention.

The New York–based artist and designer Jason Eppink is known for his street art interventions like screens which fit over illuminated advertising panels, transforming them from commercial messages into pleasant, softly-pixelated art. But his most famous project to date was a reaction to a leaky pipe in Astoria, New York. The valve, located outside an Amtrak station, had been spewing water across a sidewalk for twenty years. In summer, it was a stinky nuisance; in winter, it was an icy deathtrap. For two decades, wasted water seeped onto the street. For two decades, local residents had complained. But Eppink and his friend, fellow street artist Posterchild didn't complain. In one afternoon, using sourced materials reclaimed from the neighborhood, they designed and installed the Astoria Scum River Bridge, a seven-foot span wooden bridge that created safe passage over the urban drip.

The solution—simple in its brilliance, hilarious in its execution (they even added a cheeky dedication plaque to the front)—was so appreciated that New York council member Peter F. Vallone, Jr., presented the duo with a special commendation from the city. Two days later, Amtrak began work to fix the pipe. Within three months of the Astoria Scum River Bridge's installation, it was returned to the curb, its service no longer needed.

How many people complained about the pipe to Amtrak? How many people called that council member? How many people ruined their shoes in the ooze? How many people fell, flat out, on the iced-over concrete polka-dotted with gum, dropping their groceries, their laptops, their dignity? How many people spent hours fuming, the rest of their day ruined, but did nothing? Until one person—a designer—got fed up. But, more importantly, he got to work.

Start right there in your neighborhood. Walk until you see bad kerning and broken windows and scum rivers and people who really should be able to afford health care. Walk until you get mad. Really mad. Seethingly, spine-tinglingly mad.

And then go home and make something beautiful.

Alissa Walker is a freelance writer in Los Angeles. She writes about design, architecture, cities and transportation for publications including *Fast Company, GOOD, Dwell, Print, ReadyMade, The Architect's Newspaper*, Design Observer, Core77, and *LA Weekly*. She is associate producer for the public radio show "DnA: Design and Architecture," hosted by Frances Anderton. Alissa lives in a royal blue house in the Silver Lake neighborhood of Los Angeles, where she throws ice cream socials, tends to a drought-tolerant garden, writes infrequently on her blog, Gelatobaby, and relishes life without a car.

works/san josé
451 south 1st street
san josé, california 95113
is your community
art and performance
center—a non-profit
creative laboratory
dedicated to providing
an environment where
artists, audience, and
ideas interact to expand
the scope of cultural
and artistic experience. **works**

WAKE UP, AMERICA!

A
SINGLE
NON-REVOLUTIONARY
WEEKEND
IS
INFINITELY

185

183

09-24
MICHAEL FOX AND JUINTO
FOX LIN INC

10-04
KELLER EASTERLING
YALE UNIVERSITY

10-08
DAVID BAKER
DAVID BAKER + PARTNERS
ARCHITECTS

193

182

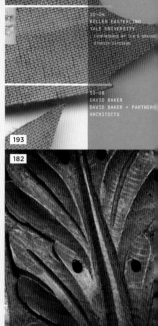

SUPPORTING

SEEKING

ORGANIZING

TEACHING

REACTING

CELEBRATING

194

rsation

7:30pm

usic

While much of this book has been organized around the designer's *relationship* to a given issue or cause—whether they seek, support or react to it—our final section makes room for work that simply celebrates. Here we acknowledge work that raises the profile of art and design. Whether in the form of a public campaign, a cross-cultural collaboration or design retrospective, whether a personal project or a grand gesture, each of these projects exists to preserve legacy and advance the cause of good design.

In her essay *Winner*, Alice Bybee shares her perspectives on the importance of celebrating, as learned from her experiences creating the groundbreaking do-gooder design competition cause/affect.

Jewish Community Center
of Greater Vancouver

950 West 41st Avenue
Vancouver | British Columbia
T. 604 257 5111
www.jccgv.com

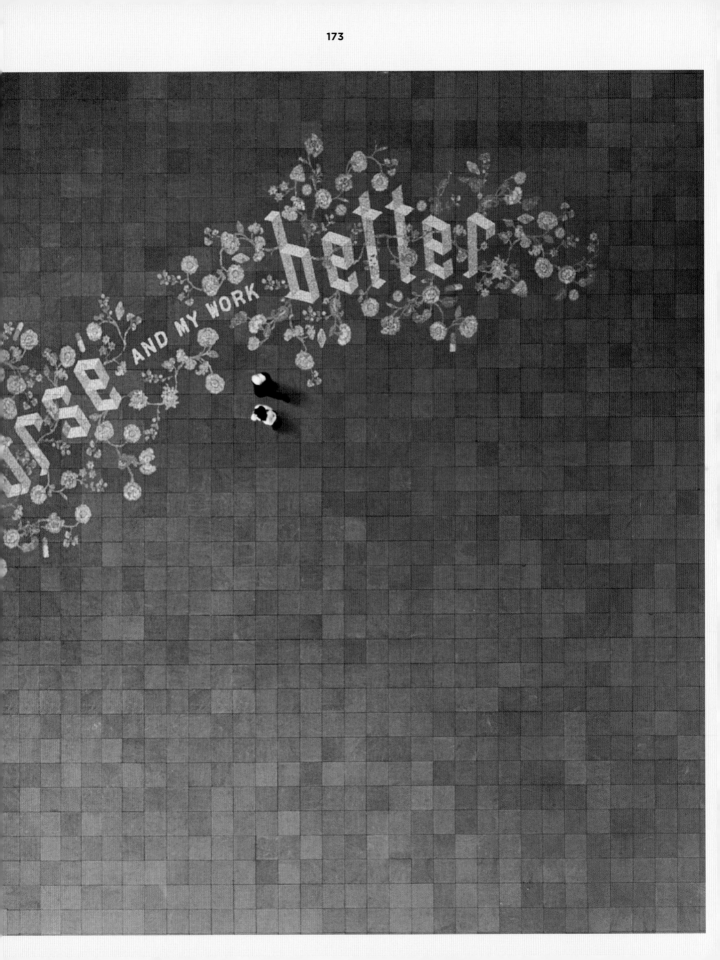

PREVIOUS SPREAD

◀ Urban Play

In 2008, Droog partnered with creative director and global collaborator Scott Burnham for a project called "Urban Play." The premise? Engage the idea of urbanism by inviting artists and designers to create public works. Would the works endure? Would they be vandalized or stolen? In a piece that ended up being emblematic of the experiment, Stefan Sagmeister's "Obsessions make my life worse and my work better" provided the answers. Constructed over eight days with the help of 150 volunteers who meticulously placed 250,000 euro cent coins, the calligraphic street work was short-lived. Shortly after it was completed, local residents noticed two men presumably stealing coins from the artwork. Police arrived on the scene and, in an effort to protect the work, swept up the coins for safekeeping. Despite its fleeting existence, this work still managed to celebrate the best in human nature: creative collaboration, volunteerism, and an underlying optimism that the beauty would not be disrupted for chance at $35,000 in loose change.

PREVIOUS SPREAD

Obsessions Make My Life Worse and My Work Better
Sagmeister, Inc. NEW YORK, NEW YORK

ART DIRECTOR Stefan Sagmeister   DESIGNERS Richard The, Joe Shouldice
CLIENT Urban Play/Experimenta

WHY YOU SHOULD CARE   It is beautiful… then gone… (Martin Venezky)

Goodlifer
Goodlifer BROOKLYN, NEW YORK

DESIGNER Johanna Björk

WHY YOU SHOULD CARE   We must replace the name "beautiful" by the name "good." (Philippe Starck)

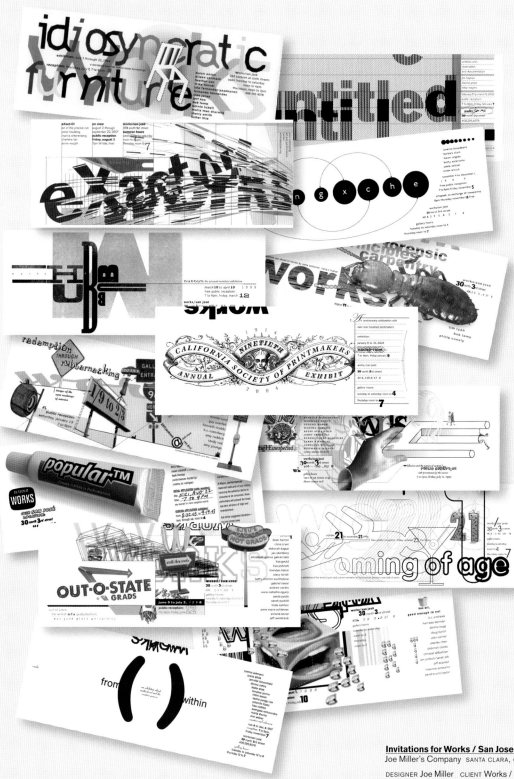

◂◂ Goodlifer

Goodlifer (www.goodlifer.com) is a community website that dares to ask, "What is the good life?" It stems from the premise that the pace of our modern lives—both personal and professional—has resulted in an unhealthy imbalance in day-to-day living. By highlighting positive examples of people, companies and products, Goodlifer aims to demonstrate that it is possible to enjoy the comforts and indulgences of a modern (Western) lifestyle, without desecrating the planet or short-changing the future. The site pulls examples and holds up heroes from a generous spectrum of modern experience. Features on food run from artisan marshmallows to local nut farms. There are investigations into sustainable investing, crowd sourcing and carrot mobbing. New ideas are mixed with old; radical notions live right alongside basic common sense. In essence, Goodlifer is an open-source guidebook to living well by living good.

◂ Works

Every month for the past 21 years Joe Miller has designed an exhibition announcement for Works, a member-supported program whose mission is to serve underrepresented artists and communities. Every one of them was created pro bono (and with a production budget of just $200 per announcement).

Invitations for Works / San Jose
Joe Miller's Company SANTA CLARA, CALIFORNIA
DESIGNER Joe Miller CLIENT Works / San Jose

WHY YOU SHOULD CARE Critical dialogue elevates practice.

win

Alice Bybee

Co-founder, cause/affect
President, AIGA San Francisco

When we started throwing around the idea of a competition for socially impactful design, the contest itself was a means to an end. Our main goal was to see if there was a community of people out there doing this kind of work that we could unite, applaud, and then work with in the future toward the common good.

Created in 2007 for the San Francisco chapter of the AIGA, cause/affect was one of the first design competitions to celebrate the work of designers and organizations who set out to positively impact our society. The competition offered an ideal forum to officially recognize, as well as to celebrate, the kind of work that often doesn't get the attention it deserves.

We wanted to shine a light on designers doing work for social good in spite of the numerous barriers they face, and inspire each other to keep up the good fight.

For many, the term do-gooder is associated with naiveté and superficial ideals. From what I've seen, do-gooder designers are quite the opposite. They are the visionaries of our field, and they are setting the bar for those who follow.

Not just another pretty face.
There was no model for how to execute or judge a design contest that was about more than just aesthetics. Not only were the merits of visual design being judged, but how successful a piece or project had been in its goal to support social good was considered as well. Was it just another pretty face, or did it have the brawn and brains to back it up?

Entry categories were initially based on how most other design contests were run, by design medium—websites, print, etc. It became apparent as the work poured in that this would have done a disservice to the layers of meaning and unique impact intrinsic in design for social good. The effectiveness of the message and objective of the design were much more important considerations, so typical categories just wouldn't cut it.

Work was recategorized by cause—community development, health and welfare, arts, education, politics and environment—websites up against brochures, logos in the same pool as posters. This made judging on aesthetics all the more difficult, and the conversations about the work much more interesting. It was no longer good enough to have a nice-looking poster; the judges wanted to know if your piece achieved its goal. This was not design for vanity's sake: You had to be worth your salt on all levels to be declared a winner.

Do it yourself.
Besides having to reconsider how design is categorized and evaluated, another break from the norm was the prevalence of self-initiated projects. Designers are tackling local and global issues they feel passionate about, using design as their tool. Whether it be access to clean water in a foreign country or public health and safety in our own communities, designers are making the time and finding the funding to engage in meaningful work outside of their day jobs. They are making the greater population aware, raising money for their cause of choice, taking matters into their own hands.

It's a win-win.

More and more people can spot soulless design from a mile away. When it comes to judging the effectiveness of design for social good, it is quite clear that the stakes are higher. As we hold ourselves accountable for more than just showcasing design standards, we begin to prioritize and laud the intent and end results.

It was clear to us then that if we are going to make a difference in our society, we needed to recognize the great strides designers have already made. But more importantly, we needed to get like-minded designers together and figure out how we can work toward the greater good. Since the inception of cause/affect, partnerships have been formed and new projects have been hatched, all out of a shared belief that we must move beyond talking about making changes; we need to get out there and do something.

It seems strange today that it was atypical to celebrate the work of designers doing socially impactful work. Now design competitions are changing the way they evaluate entries— does it inspire or engage the audience? Large consumer brands and corporations are seeing the value in funding socially responsible initiatives. Design firms are also being judged on whether or not they give back to their communities.

Design can educate, garner support and organize people. We aren't saving the world, but we are taking an active role in raising awareness and encouraging action. We have the power to make a difference, and that is what cause/affect celebrates.

Alice Bybee is a passionate advocate for nonprofits and social responsibility. After making the move from full-time do-gooder to graphic designer, she used her in-depth knowledge of design for social good to create AIGA San Francisco's Social Impact Chair and cause/affect, the graphic design competition for do-gooders. She has spearheaded projects for The Marine Mammal Center, Boys and Girls Club SF, de Young Museum and The North Face, among others.

Alice is Design Director at Iron Creative and president of AIGA San Francisco, the professional association for design.

Cause/Affect Poster ►

In 2007, designers Alice Bybee and Matt Cooke had a realization. They recognized that designers—almost by definition but certainly by training—had a propensity for doing good work for good causes. They also noticed that these projects often went unrecognized by the major design annuals. Not content to let good deeds go unnoticed, they conceived and launched a competition through AIGA San Francisco called *cause/affect*. It was the first major design awards program explicitly for "do-gooders," and it was an instant hit. "Entries poured in from all over the world," says Cooke, "We knew there were do-gooders out there, but we didn't anticipate just how universal this notion of designing for positive change really was." Bybee, now president of the San Francisco chapter, adds, "Nor how deeply felt." Today, the biennial program—along with AIGA SF's Compostmodern conference (p.102)—has become a hallmark of the chapter's progressive outlook and symbol of its commitment to social engagement.

AIGA 25th Anniversary Book ►►

To celebrate the 25th anniversary of the San Francisco chapter of AIGA, the organization created a commemorative book for its members. The book tells the story of the chapter from its founding by a few passionate individuals to its position today as the most active, innovative and looked-to organization in the 65-chapter network. As AIGA seeks to offer leadership to the profession, and as the San Francisco chapter continues to be a leading influence on that leadership, it is critical to be informed of the chapter's history, to honor the legacy of its founders and many volunteer leaders, and to be reminded of the meaningful impact the chapter has had on its members. The book was produced pro bono and distributed free to all members.

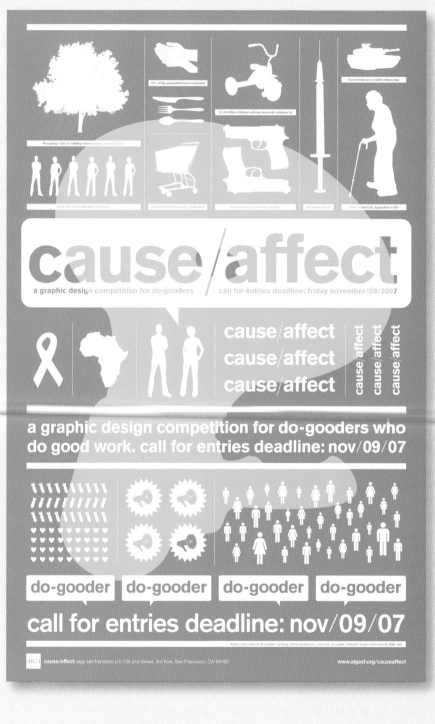

Cause/Affect Poster

Iron Creative SAN FRANCISCO, CALIFORNIA

DESIGNERS Alice Bybee and Matt Cooke
CLIENT AIGA SF

WHY YOU SHOULD CARE   You can never thank people enough. (Jeff Zucker)

AIGA SF 25th Anniversary Book

Weymouth Design SAN FRANCISCO, CALIFORNIA

ART DIRECTOR Bob Kellerman
DESIGNERS Arvi Raquel-Santos, Jenny Pan, Shasta Garcia
CLIENT AIGA San Francisco

WHY YOU SHOULD CARE   It's a free, *printed book* from AIGA!

Better Housing Coalition Awards ▶

When the Better Housing Coalition turned to Another Limited Rebellion to design an award, they probably didn't anticipate receiving four original sculptures in return. The program wanted to honor four individuals who were transforming unfinished spaces into affordable dwellings. Inspired by their example, designer Noah Scalin visited each of the four sites and scavenged unused materials to transform into trophies. The results are four distinct, humorous and personally meaningful trophies that truly celebrate the honorees' work.

On Procession ▶▶

On Procession is not just another art exhibition. It is a giant art parade. But it's not just another parade either. Participants—some commissioned artists and some from the open community—are divided into two groups that march toward each other. The two "brigades" ultimately converge on a freeway overpass (the very overpass that gave Indiana its nickname "Crossroads of America") at which point each group makes a full loop, then continues to the starting point of the opposing brigade. As they pass each other, members can fall in behind the counter procession (resulting in an infinite loop) or simply defect to the other brigade, resulting in an undefined mass of artists and spectators. To help support this unique celebration, the designers created an event identity across a range of applications ranging from balloons to banners to brochures. A 120-page book also documents the event.

Better Housing Coalition Awards

Another Limited Rebellion RICHMOND, VIRGINIA

DESIGNER Noah Scalin CLIENT Better Housing Coalition

WHY YOU SHOULD CARE It's personal.

On Procession Exhibition Catalog

Elasticbrand, LLC NEW YORK, NEW YORK

DESIGNERS Arjen Noordeman, Christie Wright CLIENT Rebecca Uchill

WHY YOU SHOULD CARE Chaos is a friend of mine. (Bob Dylan)

TWISTA ▶

This brochure is aimed at transexual/ transgender women of color—a group that has one of the highest statistical risks of HIV infection. By showcasing examples of positive role models from within the trans community, the publication encourages transgender and gender-questioning youth to participate in an ongoing support program. The program provides peer dialogue and resources that help keep these young people out of the sex industry and other destructive environments. Firebelly met directly with program leaders and participants to gain empathy for their stories and histories. The result is a narrative that is compelling and authentic—and, most importantly, effective.

2008xoxoxox68 ▶▶

Mai 68 remains the largest general strike in history. Nearly 11 million workers refused to work for two weeks, nearly toppling (but ultimately strengthening) the de Gaulle regime. To celebrate the 40th anniversary of this pivotal moment in French history, designer Brian Ponto initiated a project to reframe the movement's ideals within a contemporary context. Many parallels existed between 2008 and 1968—the destructive advance of industry, unpopular wars, conservative governments and the exploitation of patriotism among them. Ponto invited fellow artists and designers to re-imagine the enduring words and images from that tumultuous time in a simple but powerful broadsheet.

TWISTA
Firebelly Design CHICAGO, ILLINOIS

CREATIVE DIRECTOR Dawn Hancock   ART DIRECTOR Will Miller
COPYWRITER Antonio Garcia   PHOTOGRAPHER Kyle)
CLIENT Broadway Youth Center

WHY YOU SHOULD CARE   It approaches an at-risk community with honesty and dignity.

08 ×o×o× MAY68

Artists:
JODY BARTON
SCOTT BOYLSTON
SEYMOUR CHWAST
SUN DAWANG
GWENAËLLE GOBÉ
JOSH MACPHEE
FINN NYGAARD
BRIAN PONTO
U.G. SATO
CHRIS STAIN
JAMES VICTORE
BRETT YASKO
JOHN YATES

Compiled and designed by
the Studio of Brian Ponto
www.brianponto.com

These original poster prints are free to
distribute and hang. No reproductions
can be made without written permission
from the artist(s). Printed in the USA.

68 was an explosive, creative and legendary year. Many student activists believed that 1968 was the start of a world wide revolution. Almost four decades before 2003, when the Internet helped coordinate the participation of between 10 and 40 million people in simultaneous world wide demonstrations against the Iraq War, there was 1968, the year that student-led protests erupted around the world. Whether protesting the Viet Nam War or domestic repression—and often linking the two—protestors in Chicago, Mexico City, Paris, Prague, Tokyo and many other cities were tear gassed, clubbed and shot. The death tolls in Mexico City are still disputed. The one thing is not disputed, is the importance of graphics to publicize the demands and grievances. Hundreds of posters anonymously produced by artists and students were plastered all over Paris and other cities. Those produced through the Atelier Populaire were the most widely distributed and are the best known to-day. Their power, simplicity and directness communicated the students' demands, and helped forge solidarity with French workers. The brief but almost mythical French student-worker alliance led to a general strike throughout France by ten million French workers, roughly two-thirds of the French workforce.

The posters of Paris 1968 inspired—and in some cases were directly copied—by students and artists across the world. Forty years later they continue to inspire. Forty years later, there is another unpopular and devastating war, countless workers are still exploited, human rights abuses abound and many governments are more powerful and repressive than ever. The posters in this portfolio make direct reference to the rawness and forcefulness of the posters of Paris '68. They also speak directly to contemporary issues. If a poster makes you think about the world, it has achieved its goal. If a poster makes you think about the world a little differently, inspires action, moves you to publicly post them or makes you want to design your own poster, it has exceeded its goal.

There has never been a movement for social change without the arts—music, poetry, theater, posters— being central to that movement. Posters are one of the most accessible and democratic art forms. They can educate, agitate and inspire. We need powerful graphics now more than ever, as a weapon in the ongoing struggle for peace with justice. —*Carol A. Wells*

Founder and Executive Director Center for the Study of Political Graphics
Los Angeles, California. www.politicalgraphics.org

2008xoxoxox68
Studio of Brian Ponto BROOKLYN, NEW YORK

ART DIRECTOR Brian Ponto ARTISTS Jody Barton, Scott Boylston, Seymour Chwast, Sun Dawang, Gwenaëlle Gobé, Josh Macphee, Finn Nygaad, Brian Ponto, U.G. Sato, Chris Stain, James Victore, Brett Yasko, John Yates
CLIENT Self-initiated / CSPG

WHY YOU SHOULD CARE Art is a weapon of war.

"Creative for the sake of being creative is fine, but here, the creative has to serve the mission."

—Diana Berno

LANCE ARMSTRONG FOUNDATION

SURVIVAL OF THE FITTEST

AS THE IN-HOUSE ART DIRECTOR at the Lance Armstrong Foundation, Diana Berno stewards one of the most iconic brands in the world. In that capacity, she designs and manages a range of internal and external communications, including environmental graphics and conference materials for the organization's LIVESTRONG Summits, fundraising case statements, annual reports, logos, stationery, even cycling jerseys. Berno is also responsible for the design and ongoing supervision of signage and event graphics for the foundation's primary grassroots fund raiser, the LIVESTRONG Challenge, which in 2010 raised more than $8 million.

Despite seven-figure successes and the high-profile nature of her work (Berno has designed for events featuring senators John Kerry and John McCain, Dr. Sanjay Gupta, and numerous government ministers, dignitaries and executives from around the world), she is diligently sensitive to the foundation's nonprofit status. She often designs simple, two-color pieces and looks for opportunities to run multiple jobs together to save money. "People look at the bottom line of LIVESTRONG's fund raising and see a big number," she says, "What they don't always see is that every dollar represents a personal stake in the fight against cancer. Most of our expenditures go toward services for cancer survivors and their families. I have responsibility to get the maximum impact from every dollar." As an advocate for the value of design, Berno says she is also careful to limit her requests for pro bono work and services.

Working within the constraints of budget and brand also fosters a different kind of creativity. "Everything we do has to serve the mission," she explains, "When we find new ways of solving communications problems or being effective within a budget, then I know we've arrived at a truly creative solution—one that has a real and positive impact on the lives of others."

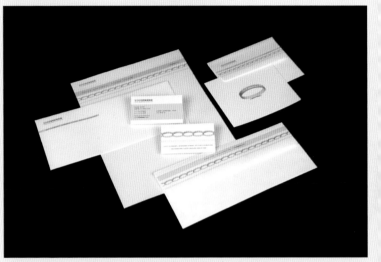

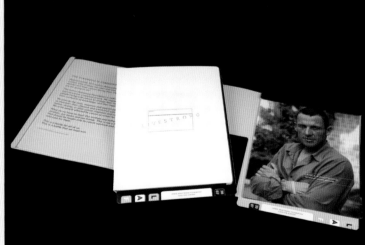

LIVESTRONG Materials
Lance Armstrong Foundation & idea21   AUSTIN, TEXAS

ART DIRECTORS Diane Berno, Tom Berno, Jeff Davis
DESIGNERS Diane Berno, Tom Berno, Jeff Davis
CLIENT Lance Armstrong Foundation

WHY YOU SHOULD CARE   No one ascends alone. (Lance Armstrong)

KUB Anniversary Brochure
Sagmeister, Inc. NEW YORK, NEW YORK

ART DIRECTOR Stefan Sagmeister   DESIGNER Joe Shouldice
CLIENT Kunsthaus Bregenz

WHY YOU SHOULD CARE   It risks.

◄◄ KUB Anniversary Brochure

The Kunsthalle Bregenz is one of Europe's most successful contemporary arts centers. The center is located in Sagmeister's hometown of Bregenz (the wealthy capital of Austria's western-most state) against the backdrop of a highly conservative political landscape. To celebrate the center's 10th anniversary, Sagmeister and crew hijacked an original issue of the local (and well-distributed) conservative newspaper, overprinting the brochure on its pages. Handling the brochure turns the reader's hands blacker and blacker, an effect the designer says is "a sly on the dominant political party." The party's official color is black.

◄ The Seattle Poster Show

The Seattle Poster shows are a series of cross-cultural design exhibitions. The exhibitions pair work by Seattle-based artists alongside that of artists and designers from foreign capitols—so far Moscow, Tehran and Havana. The poster shows are a self-initiated project by Command Z's Daniel Smith, whose aim is to celebrate diverse visual cultures and engender a form of citizen-to-citizen diplomacy—even as the governments of the participating nations (including the U.S.) isolate and demonize one another. But, says Smith, "Designers are their own tribe." Indeed, the poster shows transcend politics and break down the artificial cultural barriers that have been constructed between largely unknown "adversaries."

The Seattle Poster Show Exhibit Catalogs
Command Z SEATTLE, WASHINGTON

DESIGNER Daniel R. Smith

WHY YOU SHOULD CARE Design can go where others fear to tread.

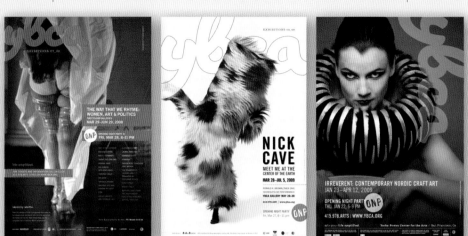

"Part of the success of the YBCA brand and its system is that it can outlive its creator."

–Cinthia Wen

YERBA BUENA CENTER FOR THE ARTS

LIFE AMPLIFIED

THE YERBA BUENA CENTER FOR THE ARTS (YBCA) is known as San Francisco's premier contemporary art and performance venue. Its location opposite the San Francisco Museum of Modern Art is an apt metaphor for the cultural space it occupies within the city. Known for its inventive and sometimes daring curatorial spirit and an unwavering commitment to diversity and relevance, YBCA offers a unique artistic lens through which we see our own connection to the world more clearly. Although this has long been the essence of what YBCA is, for years this truth was obscured behind a trendy and ultimately shallow identity. Then they connected with NOON.

Following a comprehensive brand audit, NOON developed a new tagline for the organization, capturing their mission and value in two simple words: *Life Amplified.* Those two words, crafted by writer Craig Woodgate, did more than define the institution; they became the platform upon which all of the visual branding would be based. NOON worked closely with the organization to capture and distill their story into one that was both consistent and

YBCA Branding (this page & center)
NOON SAN FRANCISCO, CALIFORNIA

ART DIRECTOR Cinthia Wen DESIGNERS Cinthia Wen, Do Young Ahn, Tomonari Ito, Claudia Fung, Hope Meng, Leah Koransky, Yoann Resmond, Ed O'Brien
CLIENT Yerba Buena Center for the Arts

WHY YOU SHOULD CARE   A good idea provides a framework for design decisions, guiding the work. (Ellen Lupton)

compelling. They recommended the moniker "YBCA" and developed a graphic language to individuate the performance, exhibitions, film, membership and community programs. NOON's branding system, like the institution, was bold and expressive but also tremendously versatile, allowing it to be applied with equal facility to catalogs, postcards, kiosk posters, ads, billboards street banners and books (all of which they produced). The look and language of the YBCA identity program soon permeated the cultural corridors of the city and the organization saw significant increases in membership and attendance.

After a transformational five-year run, a new design firm is now at the reins. Building on the foundation set by their predecessor, Volume, Inc. has brought new energy, humor and irreverence to the visual expression of the YBCA brand. Combining generic stock photography with their own urgent editorial illustration, Volume's campaign presents YBCA's case with a more aggressive voice as the institution continues to explore new avenues of expression and engage with an ever-widening audience.

YBCA 2009 Promotional Campaign (top right)
Volume Inc. SAN FRANCISCO, CALIFORNIA

ART DIRECTORS Adam Brodsley, Eric Heiman DESIGNERS Adam Brodsley, Eric Heiman, Talin Wadsworth, Kim Cullen ILLUSTRATOR Jasper Wong CLIENT Yerba Buena Center for the Arts

WHY YOU SHOULD CARE Design is an opportunity to continue telling the story, not just to sum everything up. (Tate Linden)

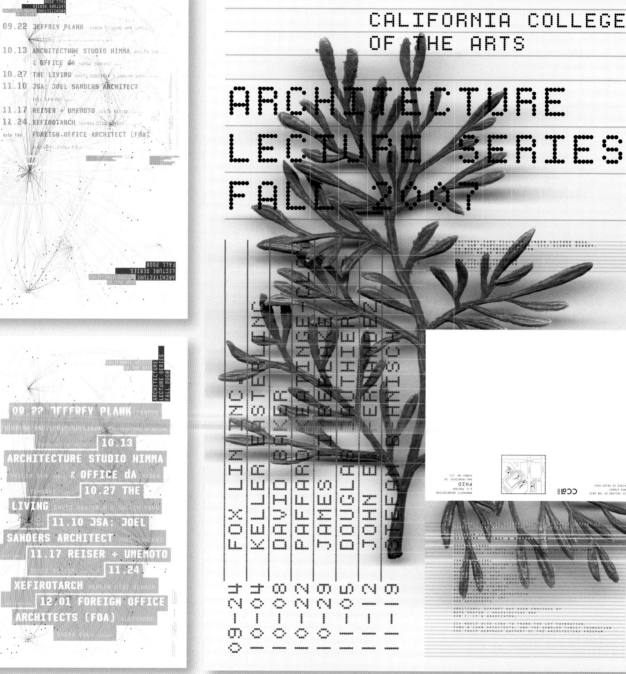

CCA Architecture Lecture Series Fall 2008, 2007

Aufuldish & Warinner SAN ANSELMO, CALIFORNIA

DESIGNER Bob Aufuldish
CLIENT California College of the Arts Architecture program

WHY YOU SHOULD CARE   Design is not making beauty. Beauty emerges from
selection, affinities, integration, love. (Louis Kahn)

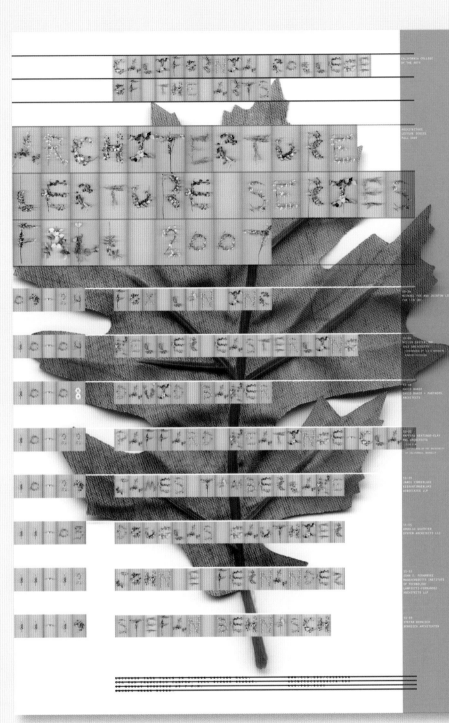

◄ Announcing Architecture

Through lectures, conferences and symposia, colleges and universities keep their fields of study critical and relevant. This set of posters from the California College of the Arts' Architecture Lecture Series promotes exactly this kind of engagement. The series, which tackles issues of architecture and global practice, shares diverse perspectives from practitioners and educators from across the United States. In what may be seen as a critical perspective on that challenge, the typography on the 2007 edition was created from silk flowers. The 2008 version, meanwhile, highlights the significance of connection.

Camp Wannadoodle ▸

Camp Wannadoodle is a nonprofit art camp that kids attend while their parents attend local design club meetings. The mark for the camp was first created by designer Meta Newhouse and was later named by copywriter Wayne Geyer—both working pro bono. The whimsically nostalgic name breathes life and humor into an already intelligent logo. The chance collaboration combined the efforts of two creative professionals to produce a result greater than the sum of its parts. Unfettered by fees, committees or "ownership" over the project, the entire identity was completed in just a few days.

Jewish Book Festival ▾

There's an economy of form present in this clever mark. Leveraging the formal similarity of a menorah and an open book creates a memorable double entendre while remaining somewhat humble. In one instance it captures the wit, reverence and sophistication of Jewish literature.

National Novel Writing Month ▸▸

This beautiful two-color offset poster celebrates a noble ambition—write a novel in just 30 days. Although the effort started in 1999 with just 21 participants, it has since grown to include more than 200,000 writers annually. For every aspiring writer who has dreamt of completing their masterpiece but didn't know where to start, the answer is now November. Emphasizing quantity over quality (50,000 words is a lot to get down in a month), NaNoWriMo wants participants to just have fun and inspire each other. The metallic gold fingerprints dotted across the iconic typewriter in Jason Munn's poster artfully exemplify this can-do attitude.

CHERIE SMITH JCCGV

JEWISH BOOK FESTIVAL

Camp Wannadoodle
Meta Newhouse Design BOZEMAN, MONTANA

DESIGNER Meta Newhouse
CLIENT Dallas Society of Visual Communications

WHY YOU SHOULD CARE With a good concept, good design sometimes comes together quickly.

Cherie Smith Jewish Book Festival
Seven25. Design & Typography. Inc. VANCOUVER, CANADA

ART DIRECTOR Isabelle Swiderski DESIGNERS Jaime Barrett, Joel Shane, Isabelle Swiderski CLIENT Greater Vancouver Jewish Community Centre

WHY YOU SHOULD CARE It's dignified without taking itself too seriously.

National Novel Writing Month
The Small Stakes OAKLAND, CALIFORNIA

DESIGNER Jason Munn
CLIENT National Novel Writing Month

WHY YOU SHOULD CARE It encourages the dream.

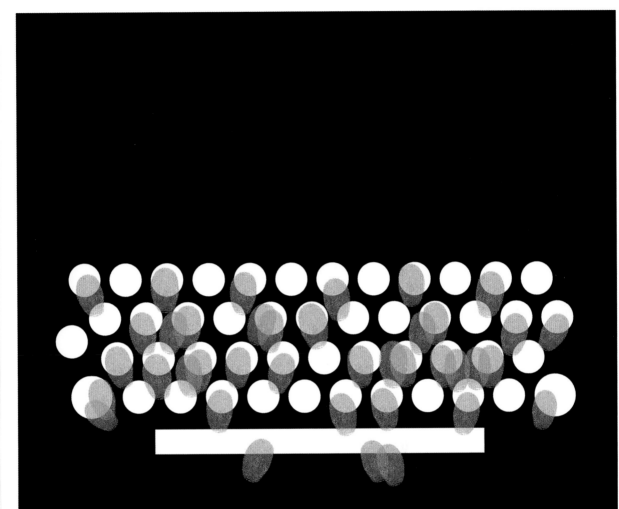

NOVEMBER

NATIONAL NOVEL WRITING MONTH

THIRTY DAYS AND NIGHTS OF LITERARY ABANDON.

Christopher Simmons

The author

Okay, so now what?

Throughout this book—and indeed throughout the process of writing it—I've tried to explore some of the many ways in which designers ply their craft in service to the greater good.

Printed, bound and now in your hands, it exists as a frozen document; a snapshot of how design engaged the issues and causes of this time. It is a celebration of good work motivated by good intentions, but it is also incomplete; it lacks your voice and your work. And so I challenge you to put down this book, pick up whatever tool you're most effective with, and use it to be excellent and—more importantly—to be good.

These are the people who inspired me to write this book.

Check out these other great titles from HOW Books!

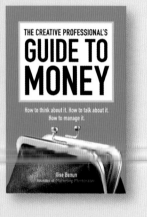

The Creative Professional's Guide to Money
Ilise Benun

Creative Workshop
David Sherwin

Box Bottle Bag
Andrew Gibbs

Learn to Manage Your Money Successfully
Not only is there much misinformation regarding money and apprehension in dealing with it, but it's also a subject that is mostly taboo. People working in creative fields don't talk about it and are afraid to reveal their ignorance or share their secrets with potential competitors. As a result, they may not know how to handle money or what financial techniques will help them succeed.

The Creative Professional's Guide to Money provides a collection of tools and ideas that will address financial questions common to many creatives.

80 Creative Challenges to Improve Your Creativity
Have you ever struggled to complete a design project on time? Or felt that having a tight deadline stifled your capacity for maximum creativity? If so, then this book is for you.

Creative Workshop includes 80 creative challenges that will help you achieve a breadth of stronger design solutions, in various media, within any set time period. Exercises range from creating a typeface in an hour to designing a paper robot in an afternoon to designing web pages and other interactive experiences. Each exercise includes compelling visual solutions from other designers and background stories to help you increase your capacity to innovate.

Take a look at the very best in packaging design
Every day Andrew Gibbs seeks out and discovers the very best in packaging design for his influential blog, TheDieline.com. Here he has collected the cream of the crop—plus some additional brand-new projects—in all their full-color glory.

Box Bottle Bag contains more than 140 projects that have succeeded on many levels. The book is divided into six chapters, each one featuring a certain style of packaging design—Luxe, Bold, Crisp, Charming, Casual and Nostalgic. The wealth of inspiration found in these pages is priceless. You'll be energized to come up with your own solutions to tricky packaging conundrums in no time.

These and other HOW titles are available at your local bookstore or from MyDesignShop.com.